THE CHANGING

Headington

BOOK TWO

Christine Bloxham
and
Susanne Shatford

SERIES
NUMBER
8

Robert Boyd
PUBLICATIONS

Published by
Robert Boyd Publications
260 Colwell Drive
Witney, Oxfordshire OX28 5LW

First published 1996
Reprinted 2008

Copyright © Christine Bloxham,
Susanne Shatford and
Robert Boyd Publications

ISBN: 978 1 899536 09 2

Printed and bound in Great Britain at
The Alden Press, Witney, OX29 0YG

TITLES IN THE *CHANGING FACES* SERIES

Contents

Front cover illustration

Mick Washington can be seen receiving the Oxfordshire Senior League Cup on behalf of Quarry Nomads following their outstanding win 1-0 against Chipping Norton in April 1966. (*Courtesy of the Oxford Mail and Times*)

Acknowledgements

This series of books has become very much a 'community project' and we are grateful for the generous contributions from local people. The names of particular contributors are acknowledged beneath the relevant photographs but we would also like to thank the following for additional material.

Gwyneth Cooke for contributions from the Barton Collection.

Andy Howland, Les Bateman and Mick Brown on the history of Oxford United, John Graham and Peter Scudder from the Headington Quarry Morris Men.

Sue Baker and Mrs Webb for material and reminiscences of St. Andrew's School.

Elizabeth Boardman, Hospital Archivist and Jenny Booth from the Wingfield League.

Keith Dolton from the Quarry Nomads Football Club.

Mr Uden, Curator of the Oxford & Bucks Light Infantry and the Queen's Own Oxfordshire Hussars Museum.

Bernard Stone, Joyce Allen, Ramon Roper, Sylvia Dring, Mr. and Mrs. Peter Dring for their continuing enthusiasm and searches for photographs and reminiscences.

Adrian Shatford for photography and drawings and Alan Scragg at the Alden Press for producing excellent results from some very poor original photographs.

Lastly we would like to thank Stephanie Jenkins for proof reading.

Introduction

Having featured the geographical development of the villages of Headington, Headington Quarry and New Headington and the hamlets of Barton and Titup in Volume One of *The Changing Faces of Headington,* we have selected various topics which help to create Headington's character for Volume Two. Headington forms a microcosm of society, being influenced by and reflecting to a certain extent what is going on in the world around it. This is shown clearly in the section on Headington at war — even though it was seldom actually attacked, hospitals took in injured soldiers and schools took on evacuees from London. The organisation of the schools in Headington has been influenced by national principles, although they have developed their individual characters. The growth of the motor industry at Cowley and improvement in national living standards led to the need for more housing, so new estates such as Barton and Risinghurst were created.

Yet Headington's character developed in an individual way. Although the nature of businesses may be similar to those found elsewhere, the characters of men like Alfred Dring who set up a carrier's business which developed into a successful coach firm and John Mattock who started off as a gardener and built up a successful specialisation in roses have exerted their own influences on the area.

The people of Headington have had ample opportunity for recreational activities, with Shotover Park on their doorstep and a vast number of different clubs and societies. The Headington Quarry morris men have achieved international fame, and it was due to a chance meeting between them and Cecil Sharp that the latter began researching morris dancing. The humble Headington United football team, founded by the vicar and a local doctor, developed into Oxford United, which achieved automatic promotion into the First Division in 1996, after a chequered career.

All these aspects have been covered in this book. It is far from a complete survey, because of limitations of space and available material, but we have tried to portray the character of the area. We have used a variety of sources including published books and articles, catalogues, personal memories, Directories, school log books, St Andrew's parish magazines, maps and local newspapers, all of which combine to build up a dossier of local information.

Headington and neighbouring areas. (*Courtesy of A.J. Walker*)

Health and Hospitals

The Warneford Hospital

'Between the celebrated walk called 'Headington-Hill' and the Cowley Road, has recently been erected by subscription a large and airy lunatic asylum; no establishment of this kind in the kingdom is conducted upon a better plan, or more carefully watched over or attended to'. Pigot's Directory, 1830.

Rev. S. W. Warnford

This establishment was the first hospital to be situated in the 'healthy air' of Headington and in 1826 was known as The Radcliffe Asylum. For the sum of £24,000, a 10 acre site was acquired 'in a healthy situation', commanding pleasant views of the surrounding countryside' and an elegant house with two wings was erected. This substantial sum was raised from members of the University, the Church and the public. It was later to be renamed after its principal founder, The Rev. S. W. Warneford, for raising £10,900 of the initial sum and for giving constant support and advice. He also lent money to subsidise the poorer patients in the early days.

The hospital was intended to provide for 'the Respectable and Educated Classes of society'. Patients who could afford to pay £250-£300 per annum acquired a private bedroom, sitting room and access to the garden- courts but those who could be classed as paupers, but were ineligible for parish relief, could be admitted to 3rd class galleries for as little as a guinea entrance fee.

" *The classes of patients and the numbers of each class who have been assisted by the Asylum from its first opening, July* 13, 1826, *to* 1838.

   7 have been clergymen.
 33 of other professions.
 18 have been the wives or children of professional men.
 49 farmers, their wives or children.
155 tradesmen, their wives or children.
 95 servants, either domestic or otherwise."

  357

P.S. The Committee of Management meets every Tuesday at One o'clock at the Savings' Bank, Oxford, on which day all applications for admission and assistance will be considered. Letters of enquiry are to be addressed either to the Physician, or House Director.

Excerpt from a brochure of 1840.

An early engraving of the Asylum c. 1838. (*Oxfordshire Health Archive*)

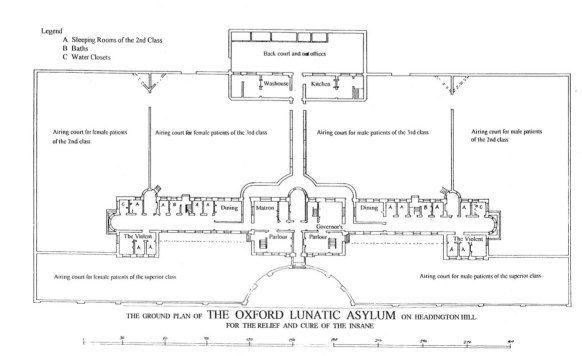

Legend
A Sleeping Rooms of the 2nd Class
B Baths
C Water Closets

Back court and out offices

Washouse   Kitchen

Airing court for female patients   Airing court for female patients of the 3rd class   Airing court for male patients of the 3rd class   Airing court for male patients
of the 2nd class   of the 2nd class

Dining   Matron   Dining

Governor's

The Violent   Parlour   Parlour   The Violent

Airing court for female patients of the superior class   Airing court for male patients of the superior class

THE GROUND PLAN OF THE OXFORD LUNATIC ASYLUM ON HEADINGTON HILL
FOR THE RELIEF AND CURE OF THE INSANE

'*The ground plan of the Oxford Lunatic Asylum on Headington Hill for the relief and cure of the insane*'. A drawing based on that of Daniel Evans, Builder, Oxford. c.1825. (*H. A. Shatford from information supplied by Oxfordshire Health Archive*)

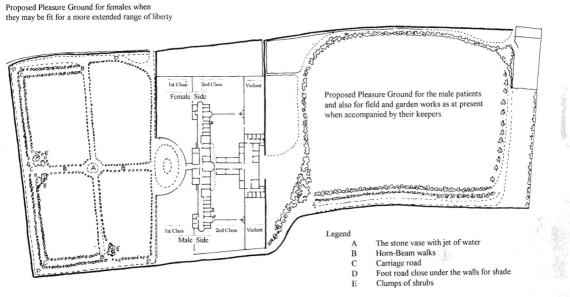

Proposed Pleasure Ground for females when they may be fit for a more extended range of liberty

1st Class 2nd Class Violent

Female Side

Proposed Pleasure Ground for the male patients and also for field and garden works as at present when accompanied by their keepers.

1st Class 2nd Class Violent

Male Side

Legend

A The stone vase with jet of water
B Horn-Beam walks
C Carriage road
D Foot road close under the walls for shade
E Clumps of shrubs

A site plan 'for the proposed pleasure grounds for patients for field and garden works when accompanied by their keepers. The hornbeam walks intersecting each other will form avenues as at Versaille'. Note the total segregation of the sexes. (*H. A. Shatford from information supplied by Oxfordshire Health Archive*)

A view of the ladies' drawing room in 1904. (*Oxfordshire Health Archive*)

The Churchill Hospital

This hospital was established in 1940 by the Ministry of Health as an emergency facility for the expected local air raids on ground owned by The Warneford. Fortunately these did not occur and when the buildings were completed in January 1942 they were leased to the American Army. The Churchill Hospital was opened by the Duchess of Kent on 27th January 1942. Oxford City Council took over the buildings when the Americans left and it was opened to civilian patients in January 1946.

The original hospital which opened in 1942 was a brick construction and provided for 600 beds. It was supplemented by a further 600 in temporary barrel shaped Nissan huts and 400 in tents. The Nissan huts have been in use until the 1990s but have now disappeared. Queen Elizabeth visited the site in July 1944. She visited the operating theatres, kitchens, recreation room and the marquee wards. She then took tea with the nursing staff in the Officers and Nurses Mess Hall.

The staff in their gas masks outside the main entrance, 1942. (*Oxfordshire Health Archive*)

The Nuffield Orthopaedic Hospital

Like the Warneford Hospital, this establishment was initiated by the perceived needs of the Radcliffe Infirmary. It started its life as a Convalescent Home (see Book 1), and was opened in May 1872.

'This institution is intended for persons who are cured, but still weak and in need of rest, good air, and wholesome food. Many a man and woman, after leaving hospital, is still unable to do a day's work; this Home provides persons with what they require in this way, who may be sent hither by the Physician or Surgeon of the Radcliffe Infirmary'. The *Headington Parish Magazine,* May 1872.

Initially the Home catered for eight patients but was enlarged during the 1st World War to cater for the convalescing wounded and in 1922 *Kelly's Directory* describes it as follows:- 'a red brick building with an annexe of two wards built of wood and iron'.

Rev John Rigaud B.D. 1821-1888, a local cleric and Don of Magdalen College, who was the driving force behind the establishment of the Convalescent Home.

It was named The Wingfield to commemorate the benevolence of Mrs Hannah Wingfield who contributed about half the funds in order to purchase the 18 acre site. Unfortunately she died in 1870 and never saw the results of her generosity.

The Convalescent Home on the left with the new nurses' home on the right. William Morris gave £70,000 in 1930 to finance the new hospital project and it was renamed the 'Wingfield Morris Hospital' in 1931, and was officially opened by H.R.H. The Prince of Wales on 30th June 1933. (*Wingfield League*)

During the First World War, the hospital was used as part of the Southern General Hospital which catered for casualties from the Western Front. There were 400 beds across the city with three bases in Headington, at the Wingfield, Churchill site (then belonging to the Warneford) and High Wall in Pullen's Lane.

Emergency wards on the Wingfield site 1914-1918. Similar accommodation was based on the Churchill site during the First and Second World Wars.

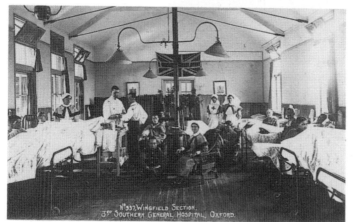

In 1917 beds were in short supply as casualties rose. Dr. Gathorne Robert Girdlestone serving with the Royal Army Medical Corps, obtained huts from the Henbury Cordite Factory near Bristol and these were erected on the site. By 1919, there were 200 beds for the treatment of post-war disabilities. Left is a view of one of the 'hut' wards. (*Wingfield League*)

The party to celebrate the end of the war in 1918 outside one of the wood and iron wards. The soldier standing by the post of the veranda is one of the orderlies, William Eagleton of 120, Lime Walk. Note the wicker spinal chair on the right for back injuries. (*Margaret Coppock*)

On 1st November 1919 the Ministry of Pensions took over the hospital from the War Office 'for the benefit of pensioners needing orthopaedic treatment' and the Wingfield as an Orthopaedic Hospital was born. Feilden Ward was retained for the treatment of crippled children and the first group of 22 patients were referred from the Radcliffe Infirmary and admitted on November 20th.

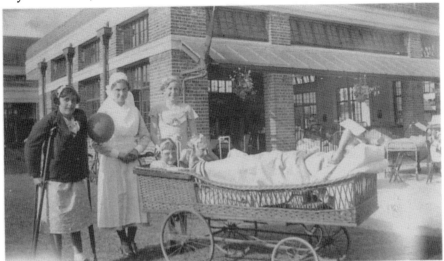

A group of patients and nurses in 1935 with two children tucked into the end of the adult wicker spinal carriage. (*Wingfield League*)

The Wingfield has been notorious for its 'fresh air' policy and this view shows patients outside in the Summer of 1932. Before the discovery of antibiotics, the only treatment for T.B. and severe infection was fresh air, good food and immobility, so patients were strapped to frames and put outside in all weathers. They received some protection from the elements by tarpaulins and stone hot water bottles but snow was often shaken off the ends of the beds and chilblains were commonplace. Nevertheless infection was reduced. (*Wingfield League*)

Mr John Snow, a ninety-year-old quarryman of 36 Pitts Road, Headington Quarry, gave £200 to the Wingfield-Morris Hospital and £200 to the Radcliffe Infirmary. This was the greater part of his life's savings. His greatest ambition was to shake hands with Lord Nuffield and he is seen above doing just that on Monday the 24th April 1930 by invitation at Cowley. (*Russell Auger*)

Headington Manor House and grounds were bought by the trustees of the Radcliffe Infirmary in 1919 to provide an extension to the city site. Sir William Osler was instrumental in raising moneys and the Red Cross contributed £15,000 from funds collected during the war. Sir William Osler died in 1919 and so did not see the fruits of his labours. In 1920 there was great pressure on beds for tuberculosis patients and the National Association for the prevention of Tuberculosis suggested that the Headington extension be used for this purpose, and plans were made to open a unit of 80 beds. The foundation stone was laid on the 24th September 1925 by Lady Osler and the Osler Pavilion was opened by Mr Neville Chamberlain, Minister for Health, on 1st January 1927 but it only accommodated 40 patients.

The proposed plan of the Headington extension on the Manor site c.1920s. (*Oxfordshire Health Archive*)

Pupils at the open air school for children with T. B. in the 1930s. One pupil who attended in the 1940s remembers working inside in the snow with only a canvas screen to protect them from the elements. (*Mr Ford*)

In the 1930s, parts of the site were sold off and the proceeds were used to extend the Infirmary; the Headington site was not developed until 1972 when the John Radcliffe Maternity Unit was opened, followed by the J. R. 2 in 1979.

St. Ebba's

John Stansfeld was born in Lincolnshire. While stationed in Oxford for Customs and Excise, he gained a degree in 1889, studying part-time at Exeter College. He was then transferred to London where he continued his studies and qualified as a Doctor at Charing Cross Hospital and worked with the poor of Bermondsey but was forced to leave due to his children's ill health in 1912. However in 1909 he had taken holy orders and came to work in the parish of St Ebbes, Oxford until 1926. He purchased the site in Quarry Road to give the families of the slums some respite in the healthy air of Headington. The chapel which stood on the site was built by unskilled labour. It was of rough stone with a thatched roof and straw on the floor. It seems to have disappeared at about the time of the 2nd World War.

The Rev. Dr. J. Stansfeld.

A view of St Ebba's Chapel showing the stocks with whipping post on the right. No-one appears to know how they came to be there or to where they have gone. (*S. Dring*)

An internal view of the chapel which was demolished in the 1950s. (*T. Williams*)

Temporary housing was put up on the site during the 1920s. The picture to the right shows the Bradshaw family outside their chalet. Building materials had been reclaimed from anywhere and everywhere, and evidence of this can see in the elaborate stained glass window that has been integrated into this home. (*J. Smith*)

The Birmingham Education Authority now leases the site as a study centre. One lad remembers coming in 1936 at the age of thirteen and says:

'It was my pleasure to learn that there was in life such things as trees and flowers, grass and fresh air and many other things removed from bricks and concrete, factories belching forth thick smoke, producing what thankfully now is a thing of the past — SMOG — a fatal mixture of fog and toxic smoke. It killed very many old and young who were unable to with stand its effects. I attended a service in the little home - made church and shook hands with Dr Stansfeld.' (Denis Murray)

Headington at War

The First World War 1914-1918.

In World War 1 the Oxford and Bucks Light Infantry Regiment expanded to 17 battalions. 5,878 Officers and other ranks gave their lives and from the 52nd Battalion only 29 of the 1,000 men returned, many being Headington lads.

A Bugle Patrol c.1918 from Joyce Webb's Family album. The Corporal can be seen on the back row left and the four seated in front are displaying medals from the war; the 1st is a Veteran Bugler, the 3rd is the Bugle Major and centre is the Adjutant. The Buglers would all have been young boys recruited as early as twelve years of age. Note the puttees worn at this time. (*J. Webb*)

The certificate of Demobilisation belonging to Private George Thomas Webb of New Headington. He had joined the Air Force and fortunately returned safely, unlike so many others.

The troops marching up the London Road past the White Horse. This was a common sight as the the ground to the north of the London Road, where Headley Way is now situated, was used as a campsite. (*Jeremy's P.C.*)

Troops passing Bury Knowle Park in 1914. Many are wearing shorts and would probably have served in Mesopotamia rather than on the Western Front. (*P. Dring*)

The War memorial in Holy Trinity Churchyard, Headington Quarry

This Memorial was erected at the end of the First World War to commemorate those from the Quarry who gave their lives for their country. Many lied about their age in order to join up. In the Church Porch is a tablet listing the 45 names shown below. (*H. A. Shatford*)

B.W. Brazier	C. J. Gurl	H. Perrin
D. J. Butler	E. Gurl	G. Prichard
J. Clare	H. Hedges	G. Skey
T. Cooper	W.G. Herbert	H. Smith
W.F. Cooper	J. Heritage	W. Smith
E. Coombes	A Horwood	P. Surman
E. C. Coppock	B. F. G. Jeffs	A. Taylor
R. Coppock	J. A. Kislingbury	A. E. Taylor
G. Cox	A. Kimber	H. J. Trafford
W. A. Cox	R. J. Kimber	W. I. Trafford
P. D. Doyne	T. G. Kimber	G. Trafford
J Drewitt	A. Marshall	J. Tolley
R. C. Eveleigh	R. Morris	W. Webb
E. C Edwards	R H. N. Prior	A. Wright
A Gurl	F. C. Parsons	C. Ward

Alfred Radburn, brother of Daisy Webb in New High Street, who joined the army at Cowley Barracks in 1915, after lying about his age. He went to France at the age of 17 and was killed the following year. (*J. Webb*)

The embroidered card was sent to his Mother in 1915. On the reverse is the message:

> '*To my Dear Mother,*
> *From her Loving Son Alfred'*
>
> (*J. Webb*)

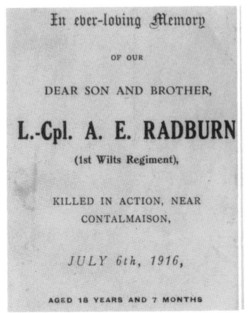

In ever-loving Memory

OF OUR

DEAR SON AND BROTHER,

L.-Cpl. A. E. RADBURN

(1st Wilts Regiment),

KILLED IN ACTION, NEAR
CONTALMAISON,

JULY 6th, 1916,

AGED 18 YEARS AND 7 MONTHS

The Memorial of Alfred Radburn's death. He was assigned to the 1st Wiltshire Regiment as that was where recruits were needed at the time of his enlistment. (*J. Webb*)

Cyril Webb from The Croft also joined up at Cowley Barracks but volunteered to join the Royal Engineers. (*D. Webb*)

Two 17 year old Headington Boys plus friend at Aldershot just before leaving for France in 1915. Rowland Morris (centre) of Old Headington was wounded twice but survived and his future brother-in-law Hubert Hall of Stile Road (right), remained in the army after the war and served in India. (*J. Allen*)

William Francis Charles Stone (seated) and Reginald Hadland serving in the Oxford and Bucks Light Infantry during the First World War (*B. Stone*)

Private William Stone's Service Certificate signed by Major R. Bannister-Crosse (archivist and historian) who was one of the 29 members of the 2nd Battalion to serve throughout the war and survive.

John Washington of Headington Quarry at some time during the 1914-18 War in the ceremonial uniform of the Oxford & Bucks Regiment. This uniform with the red jacket was originally standard dress but was latterly reserved for parades. (*D. Webb*)

The Second World War 1939-1945

Attacks from the air brought the threat of war to everyone's door and air-raid shelters were a prominent feature.

The air-raid shelter being dug in Windmill Road in 1939 on the present site of the car park at the corner of St. Leonard's Road. (*OPA*)

Rachel Groves (left) outside her Anderson Shelter now converted into a rockery. Rachel remembers her husband excavating the site and the City Council supplying the shelter. It was then equipped with blankets and emergency rations in case of a bomb raid.

The siren on Holyoake Hall would sound the warning for all to take cover. This siren was tested regularly after the war until the mid 1950s.

'We were at Barton all during the war, the blackout and the searchlights, it was very frightening. We had one of those big metal table shelters in the kitchen. We were supposed to get in there with all the kids if the siren went'

'I remember there was a big grassy bank opposite The Fox, we used to sit on that bank and watch the bombers going over, going over to bomb Coventry. We watched the planes going over sitting on that bank'. (*W. Heath*)

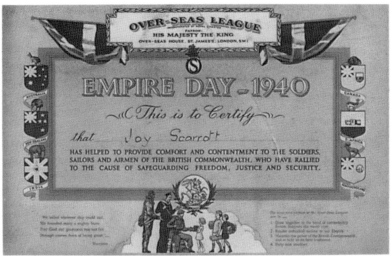

Certificate "Empire Day 1940" (*J. Scarrott*)

Joy Scarrott (now Joy Lee of Bassett Road, Barton) was 7 years old in 1940 when she received this certificate for knitting gloves and scarves for the forces.

Joy Scarrott pictured with her Mother, Martha in 1942.

Certificate of appreciation.

Martha Scarrott (now living in Henry Taunt Close, Barton) was one of the many people to receive a certificate from the Queen for taking strangers into her house when they needed accommodation.

'Not that we really had any choice, if you had any spare room, you were expected to take evacuees. We had to go down to what was the Ice Rink on Botley Road to fetch them. We had several different families, sometimes it was whole families and sometimes just the children. Several of them kept in touch for years afterwards. It was nice to get a letter from the Queen to say thank you — I always kept mine, just to show that I had a letter from Royalty.' (*Joy Scarrott*)

The Quarry W. I. making 100lbs of jam for the war effort. 30th August 1940. (*OPA*)

'Food rationing was introduced into the country by Christmas 1939. I celebrated my 21st birthday on 3rd August 1943 – my sister got married on 18th September 1943 and by giving up some points each to buy the dried fruit, we managed a small cake and also my birthday cake'. (Memories of Phyllis Cooper)

'I used to put our Basil in the front of the cake queue, and then go to the back, that way we got two lots - well you had to if you had a big family. Then we'd get six pen'orth of speck fruit so that the kids could have some fruit. Mr Jacobs at the Nursery was always good, when I was expecting and struggling up the hill to the shops at Headington, there weren't any other shops, he would always call for me to stop on the way back for a bag of apples.'

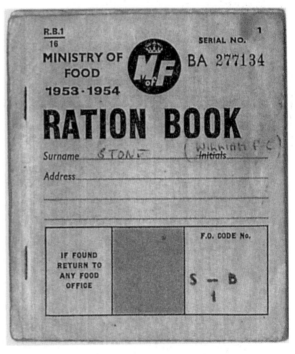

Rationing continued into the 1950s.

'I remember a delivery chap from Vallis Bakers, miserable old sod, used to come round with a horse and cart. Well I always looked after the garden, so I used to go out with my bucket and shovel to get the dung. This day he suddenly says to me, "Hey Missus — You rationed with me?" I said I wasn't so he yells at me, "Well leave my B★★★★★ dung alone then". (Vi Clark nee Peck)

'There was a frantic chase to purchase blackout material as you had to black out all lights at night. We had to cover the lights on the motor cars, buses, vans, lorries and bicycle lamps to just a small circle so it would not give a lot of light out.' (*Phyllis Cooper*)

On the right is Alfred Dring with his taxi c.1940. The headlights are covered with a black grill to prevent the lights from being seen by the enemy aircraft. (*P. Dring*)

Cyril (Pedger) Green. (*J. Maisey*)

"V" for Victory at Barton.

This V for victory still survives on the front of 22 Fettiplace Road, Barton and was placed there by Cyril (Pedger) Green in 1945. It is reputed to have been made from a piece of German aircraft.

A group from the Headington Platoon Homeguard in March 1942. Back row: Pt. Bowen, Pt. Weaver, Pt. Pulfare, Pt. Brown. Front row: Pt. Harrison, Pt. Allen, Pt. Grain, Pt. Comley, Pt. Burke.

There were celebrations everywhere at the end of the war in 1945. (*Annie Hatwell*)

Quarry Village Hall with families from Trinity Road, Quarry High St and Green Road. Names have been supplied by Harry Gurl and family.

Among the group are: Back standing: Nell Coppock, Lily Sherlock, Kate Coppock, Louie Bushnell, Annie Cooper, Mary Sheppard, Milly Baker, Mr Hobbs, Mary Kislingbury, Mrs Hobbs, Mrs Bartlett, Walter Sheppard, Eric Bishop. Front standing: Mrs. Dixon, John Brookes, Denise Benson, Mrs Benson, Mrs Horwood, Mrs Jubal Jones, Sis Phillips, Mary Coppock, Jean Brandon, Margaret Sheppard, Stan Milton. Sitting: Renie Kerry, Sonia Horwood, Doug Hobbs. Kneeling: Lily Gurl, Clare Phillips, Jean Dixon, Joan Watson, ? Jones, Roy Horwood, ? Jones, Bill Brandon, Keith Short, Chris Hathaway, Bert Baker, Lennie Short. Front: Jean Coppock, Christine Sheppard, Lennie Brandon, ? Jones, Ian Sheppard.

Gipsy Lane V. E. Day Celebration 6th May 1945. The party took place outside Nos 49, 51 and 53 the homes of the Fry, Courtnage and Devison families. (*Ramon Roper*)

Names of participants from the left clockwise round the table: Major Thorold, – Levy, Grandchild Levy, Mrs Katy Levy, Miss Fry, Martin Dorrell, Mrs Prior, Mrs Stimpson, Mr Grant, Grant's Lady Lodger, Mrs Clay, Peggy Edwin (nee Allington), Mrs Grant, Mrs Elvin, Mrs Hounslow, Mrs Moss, Mrs Hunt, a lodger, Mrs Humphris, Mrs Smith, Mrs Fry, Victor Reynolds (Smith's lodger), Charlie Goslin, ? Ernie Cooke (a billeted soldier), Mrs Richings, Mr Payne, lodger, Veronica Courtnage, Eunice Waters, Mr Dorrell, Mr Hunt, Mr Lockwood, James Lockwood, Mr Chaundy, Mr Fillis, Mrs Moss, Mr Pickford, ? – Thorold, Mrs Thorold, Rhona Chaundy, Christine Clarke, Mavis Payne, Gladys Lawrence, Evelyn Humphris, Carol Prior, Mrs Elvin's grandson, Ramon Roper, Frank Smith, Derek Chaundy, Kenneth Hall, John Pickford, Gladys Hall, Kathleen Joyce Roper, Michael Pickford, Gordon Moss, Brian Toms, Roger Chaundy, John Lawrence, Edmund Courtnage, Clifford Moss, Paddy Dawes' daughter, Paddy Dawes, Geoffrey Patrick, James Hall, John Lawrence, Margaret Moss, Betty Moss, Beryl Parker, Judith Lockwood, June Stimpson, Hazel Clay, Francis Whalley, Ruth Clay, Barbara Whalley, Daphne Minty (nee Boscott), Minty, Tony Whalley, Susan Smith, Thorold's grandchild, Misses Fry's lodger, two Thorold grandchildren, Mr & Mrs Pickford.

SECTION THREE

Sports and Leisure

The Sunday School outing c.1906 from the Baptist Chapel in Old Headington. Standing in the first carriage on the left is Alfred Dring, the carrier from Windmill Road, with his wife and daughter Edie. These events were memorable occasions for the children as outings were rare. (*P. Dring*)

Mrs Morrell's Park, now known as South Park, in 1920. The occasion is probably a Sunday School outing as one resident remembers the basket chairs being collected from All Saints Church Hall in Perrin Street and being transported by Alfred Dring to be arranged for the adults at the festivities.The afternoon consisted of sports followed by a tea party. The children received prizes. Alfred Dring can be seen on top of the lorry. (*P. Dring*)

Shotover

The name Shotover derives from the Old English *scoet ofer* or steep slope and it was part of the Royal Forest from medieval times. These forests were not necessarily woodland but areas which came under the jurisdiction of forest law. The landowner, in this case the King, controlled the use of the land and the inhabitants and enforced the forest laws through the forest courts. The killing of wild boar and game, damage to timber and brushwood, building and enclosure were all prohibited. Poachers were severely punished in the 11th century and William 1 had been known to remove offenders' eyes.

Hunting was a popular sport and it was recorded that venison from Shotover supplied the royal table at Windsor in the 13th century. The oak trees were greatly valued by the navy; in 1629 the shipwrights marked 27,000 trees as being:

'the best in the kingdome for shippinge, both for hardness and toughness thereof being not apt to rend or cleave.'

To local inhabitants, Shotover has been a valuable source of stone, timber, clay, ochre pannage for pigs, firewood and food (often poached). By 1929 it had been purchased by the University and the City Council. It is now a designated Country Park.

A group of Headington lads enjoying a walk on Shotover. c.1920. (*J. Webb*)

Throughout the 20th century, Shotover has been popular for family outings and above is a typical scene of a family walking their dog along the Ridings. c.1930. (*J. Slaymaker*)

Bertie Baker of Headington Quarry in 1946 with the three cups that he won at Tetsworth Open Horse Show and Gymkana. The horse on the left was called Sue and belonged to Joyce Morris and the one on the right was Bertie's and was called Maggot. Bertie was a talented rider and frequently rode other people's ponies to victory. His ambition was to be a jockey but he joined the family motor business instead. The horses were put out to pasture in Haynes' Field on the northern side of the by-pass. (*J. Allen*)

In the first half of this century, young people had to create their own amusement, and pictured above is a group resting after an informal game of hockey in Stowood. The sticks were cut from the trees and the group includes James Edwards, Fred Stone and Stan Currill. (*J. Pattison*)

Another group in Bury Knowle Park in 1938. Back row: — — , June James, Jimmy Hall. Front row: Ramon Roper, Clifford Moss, Edmund Courtnage, Noel Sanders. (*R. Roper*)

Public Houses

Many social activities were organised from the local pubs and below is a group from The Chequers in the Quarry just after the 2nd World War. They were going to The Derby and had stopped on route. They are from left to right. Standing: Frank Sherlock, Lilian Lawrence, Millie Baker, Mrs Ivo Gurl, – –, Mrs Brown & daughter, Ivo's sister, – –, Ivo Gurl, Gilbert Coppock. Front: – –, Margaret Coppock, Mary Kislingbury, – –, Kate –, – –. (*G. Kerry*)

The Chequers Aunt Sally Team in 1952 when they won the Oxford City League at Quarry. They were a successful team throughout the 1950s. Standing: Stan Milton, Mrs Milton, George East, Joyce Morris, Archie Morris, Rowly Morris, Chris Surman, Eddie Holland, Charlie Eden, Bill Trafford, Tingie Hall, Mrs R. Morris, Mr Meeden. Kneeling: Roy Longford, Jim Tantrum, Donald Allen with Ernie Smith (Minnie) in front. (*J. Allen*)

The 'Five-a-Side' football team outside The Chequers c.1950. Standing: Ronnie Winters, John Coppock, Maurice Bowen, Ronnie Kerry, Front: Donald Allen. (*J. Allen*)

The Men's outing from the Crown and Thistle at Titup c. 1950. These occasions usually consisted of a coach trip to the sea in one of Dring's coaches punctuated by several 'beer' stops. The happy group below include: Standing: John Diamond, Coach Driver, − −, − −, 'Curly' Cooper, 'Nibbler' Cooper, Bert Kingdom (front), − −(back), Tom Ann, 'Brasher' Parsons, − −, − −, Frank Lee (Landlord), George Kerry, 7 unknown, Owen Higginson, Walt Brigham, Bert Talbot, − −, Tom Gardner. Front: − −, − −, Jock Walsh, Billy Baker, − −, Hughie Robbins, Don Allen, Billy Currill, John Hatwell. (*G Kerry*)

Friendly Societies, The Ancient Order of Foresters

Friendly Societies were the fore-runners of the Insurance Companies and Building Societies and protected their members in times of ill health before the National Health Scheme was established in 1948. Subscriptions appear to have been collected on a monthly basis at the local pub. Below is a membership card for the Court Napoleon which was based at the Six Bells. Each Court was organised by a Management Committee of twelve which enforced the rules of the society listed below.

ANCIENT ORDER OF FORESTERS
(Oxford District)

Approved Society 152, National Health Insurance Act.

COURT 'NAPOLEON'
No. 6829

• HELD AT

The 'Six Bells' Headington Quarry

No.................   1948-49

Name ....

The Secretary cannot under any circumstances receive contributions at his residence on Court Nights.

Abstract of Local Rules and General Laws of the Order

Objects

The objects of the Court are the following—
1 Sick pay to members when ill.
2 Funeral Benefits to members.
3 Funeral benefits to members' Wives and Widows.
4 Convalescent Home Treatment.
5 Granting relief to members in distressed circumstances.

Notice

It is particularly requested that when a Brother receives this card, he will make himself acquainted with the rules therein as he will not be allowed to plead ignorance of them. The fines will be strictly enforced.

Rules

This Court shall be named ' Napoleon,' No. 6829, and shall form a branch of the Ancient Order of Foresters Friendly Society, hereinafter called ' the Order.' It shall also be connected with and form a branch of the Oxford District of the said Order for the purpose of re-assuring the lives of the members of the Court and the Wives or Widows of the said members, and for any other object provided for by the rules of the said District and the rules of the Order herein called the General Laws, and the Court shall remain in connection with the said District as a branch thereof until sanction to recede therefrom has been obtained persuant to the 43rd General Law.

Constitution and Government

This Court shall consist of an unlimited number

Social events were also organised by the Society and above is a picture of a pageant on Quarry Field, now the site of the recreation ground, c.1920. (*L. Francombe*)

Another traditional pub activity is darts and pictured above is the team at The Prince's Castle in 1968 where Dot Wilmer, left, is receiving an award from Louie Grain, the landlady. Also pictured are Joan Wilmer, Barbara Wilmer, June Maisey, Lynnette Maisey and Ernie Grain, the Publican. (*J. Maisey*)

After the 2nd World War, day outings to the sea-side became very popular and one such group can be seen above outside The Prince's Castle ready for a day at Southsea in 1968. (*J. Maisey*)

The Holyoake Hall

The hall was built by the Oxford Co-operative and Industrial Society in 1938. It was opened early in 1939 and consisted of a large dance hall with a meeting room above.
In 1926, the Co-operative Women's Guild was formed and this was followed by a similar Men's Group in 1930. Both groups originally met in the Quarry Village Hall but moved their venue to the new Guild Room in 1939.

The opening of the hall in 1939, taken from the window of Mr Williams' Bicycle Shop. The Holyoake Hall was built on the site of Holyoake Terrace and was a popular venue for dances and social events. The Blue Star Players and the Rhythmic Serenaders were two popular Groups. (*Mrs. Pontin*)

The photograph of the opening ceremony was taken from the first floor window of Williams' Bicycle Shop now the site of Hacienda. (*Mrs. Pontin*)

P. C. Griffin in Holyoake Road c. 1920. He was a popular local figure and was known to escort the young girls safely home after the dances at the Hall. (*J. Pattison*)

The British Workman's Club

This was established in 1880 at 65, Old High Street and was the headquarters of the Temperance Society. Inns and beer houses were important 'community centres' and this provided:

'A public house without the drink where man may sit, talk, read or think and sober home return.'
(*H. A. Shatford*)

The society had started in the home of Mrs Coggins in the Croft until Mrs Ballachey of Bury Knowle House gave the land for the present building.

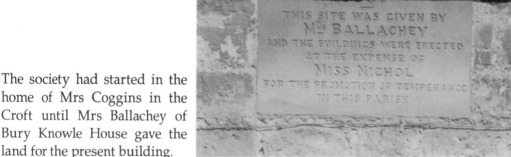

The club room at the rear of the building, erected in 1883 by Miss Watson Taylor of the Manor House, has been the venue for dances, whist drives, soup kitchens, the Girls Club, Baby Clinic, adult education classes and sports clubs. In the 1960s it was leased to the Viking Sports Club. (*H. A. Shatford*)

The Women's Institute

The Headington Women's Institute was established on 25th April 1918 and met each month at the British Workman's Club in Old High Street. The War Kitchen illustrated in Book 1 must have been one of its first initiatives. The Institute has promoted the arts and crafts in drama, music, cookery and preserving. It has been instrumental in promoting the education and interests of women throughout this century.

In 1923 the Quarry ladies decided to form their own W.I. group and have been meeting ever since. Pictured above is a group in the 1950s on an outing. Included in the photograph are Edna May Evans, Hilda Webb, Ada Luckett, Mrs. R. Morris, Mrs. Short and Meg Deards from the village shop in Pitts Road. (*J. Allen*)

The Quarry W. I. dinner at the Village Hall in the early 1950s. Mrs Morris and Mrs Luckett can be seen enjoying the occasion seated on the right. (*J. Allen*)

The Bury Knowle Club

The organisation was founded on 1st July 1933 by a group of business men who were resident in Headington. It was modelled on the London Gentlemen's Clubs and was governed by a strict code of etiquette — ladies were not admitted. The group had no political affiliation and was designed for members to meet and relax together. The premises in Windmill Road close to Headington 'Carfax', were initially leased and consisted of a bar, lounge and meeting room which was managed by an employed steward. Membership was obtained by application to the committee with references. The Club continues to operate today and women are now welcomed.

The founder members or promoters of 1933:

A. L. Shuttleworth	D. Rawlinson
C. A. J. Howard	J. S. Harris
E. J. Hall	H. E. Liversidge
W. Seddon	

Members of the Bury Knowle Club in 1965, probably taken at the annual dinner in one of the Oxford Colleges. Back Row: — Riley, Cyril Lambourne, Ted Mullis, Eddie O'Brien, Walter (Bob) Dring, Alex Steele, David Exley, Fred Evans. Front Row: Dennis Titchel, Frank Harding, Oswald (Ossie) Hunter, President, — Morris, Eric Whiting. (*P. Dring*)

Presidents
1933-1955.

D. Rawlinson
W. Seddon
Major Liversidge
A. L. Shuttleworth
J. S. Harris
E. J. Hall
G. Morris
J. Pannell
E. Sear
Aubrey Gurden
A Steele
W. Kennah
G. Hutt
C. H. A. Howard
T. Ager
H. Smith
J. Evans
W. Beaument
A. Williams
M. Cole
H. Sanger
L Bowles
F. Sear

Bob Dring, President of the Club in 1960 with his wife Nancy greeting Mr and Mrs Gurden at the annual dinner. (*P. Dring*)

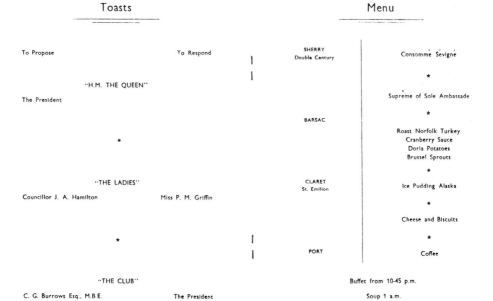

Toasts			Menu
To Propose	To Respond	SHERRY Double Century	Consommé Sévigné
			*
"H.M. THE QUEEN"			
The President			Supreme of Sole Ambassade
			*
		BARSAC	Roast Norfolk Turkey Cranberry Sauce Doria Potatoes Brussel Sprouts
*			*
"THE LADIES"		CLARET St. Emilion	Ice Pudding Alaska
Councillor J. A. Hamilton	Miss P. M. Griffin		*
			Cheese and Biscuits
			*
*		PORT	Coffee
"THE CLUB"		Buffet from 10-45 p.m.	
C. G. Burrows Esq., M.B.E.	The President	Soup 1 a.m.	

The 'Ladies Festival' dinner 30th November 1961 at the Randolph Hotel, Oxford.

The Scout Movement

The 48th Oxford Cub Pack that met in the hall next to the old Vicarage in St. Andrews Road, formerly Church Street, in 1936. Back right: Rev. Bird. Standing: John Barlow (half) three unknown, George East, John Simms, Raymond Hall, — —. Kneeling: — —,Gilbert Baker, Stan Morris, Basil Cooper, Arthur Taylor, John Webb, — —. Front: Reg Cooper, — —, Dennis Webb. — —. (*D. Webb*)

The 27th Oxford Scouts chopping wood for pensioners in the old Barton Community Centre gym in 1959. The centre was heated by the old tortoise stove which can be seen in the background. The scouts are Ken Cavanagh, Jeff Wareham, Michael King, Alan Mold and Graham Wilson. (*G. Wilson*)

Boys Brigade

After the Coronation Party in Brampton Road, Barton, there was 8/4d left in the funds and this was used by Gordon Wiggins, the organiser of the Street Party, to start the 4th Oxford Boys Brigade. On the left is Gordon Wiggins on parade leading his boys into St. Andrews School from the London Road in 1963. (*G. Wiggins*)

The 4th Oxford boys camping at Ladram Bay near Sidmouth in the 1950s. Back: Michael Phillips, Tony Weston, Ray Bushnell, Gordon Wiggins, J. McKenna, David Skyrme, – –. Front: George Peedle, P. Allen, four unknown.

Skip James leading the 49th Oxford Sea Scouts at the Drumhead Parade in 1969. (*J. Allen*)

Community Centres

The Barton Community Centre at Underhill Circus was originally a second-hand prefabricated building erected by volunteers. It was completed in 1949 and officially opened in 1950.

The Barton Community Centre Committee in 1950s. Back Row: − −, Joyce Fry. Middle Row: Rona Smith, Beryl Barson, Jane Parry, − Heath, Diane Cleary. Front Row: Zea Fry, Mrs Fleetwood, Margaret Belcher, Mrs Baines, Jean Stevenson, Ken Martin, − − . (*L. Wells*)

Botcher, June Lane, Mr. Burden, K. Ledwill, Jean Kent, Pat McLean, Mushy Goodall, Brian Embrey, Tommy Braham. (*P. Webb*).

An audience enjoying a performance at Barton in the 1950s. (*M. Tomes*)

Parties and Celebrations

The Silver Jubilee Party at Barton End in 1935. (*OPA*)

Mr H. J. Bradley lived at Barton End; he was a notable business man in Oxford in the 1930s and used to visit Humphrey Cross in Barton Village to talk about old times. He made many contributions to the community of Headington. On this occasion he provided a wonderful party in his house and garden for the residents of Barton Village and Barton Road. The children can be seen above enjoying the feast.

Memories of Coronation Day 2nd June 1953. (*M. Davies*)

The Brampton Road Coronation Party organised by Gordon and Joan Wiggins who then used the 8/4d that was left over after the celebrations to start the Boys Brigade. Above is the tea party and below are the entrants for the fancy dress parade. (*G. McLean*)

Another group celebrating outside the Community Centre in 1953. (*G. McLean*)

The Quarry Nomads

No-one seems to remember exactly how the Quarry Nomads first started but the team initially developed from a group of keen football enthusiasts in the mid 1930s. When they were considering a name for the team, some one suggested 'The Nomads' and everyone agreed. Mr. Richards, the Headmaster of Quarry School is alleged to have commented,

'Why **NOMADS?** *You haven't been anywhere.'*

Before the war, the team was organised by Mr K. Bishop and after the war, V. Coppock took over.

The Quarry School Football team in 1933, later to become the foundation of the Nomads. Back: L. Washington L. Robbins,G. Wright, R. Coppock, V. Morris, F. Hooper, – Hooper. Front: H. Wright, F. Wharton, T. Boyce, B. Green, S. Surridge. (*K. Dolton*)

One of the first teams in 1937, pictured on the Quarry Recreation Ground, where they have always practised. Back: J. Smith, T. Bartlett, S. Bagnell, J. Cook, Laurie Washington, D. Bagnell C. Walker, F, Washington. Front: F. Hooper, F. Wharton, G. Wright, H. Smith, B. Green, R. Green. (*K. Dolton*)

The team in 1949-50 outside the Chequers, when they won the Junior Cup. Back Row: Benny Benfield (landlord), Derek Hunter, George Baker, Modgy Bowen, John Hatwell, Donald Allen, Bill Washington (manager). Front Row: Denny Enstone, Albert (Nibbler) Cooper, Phil Harrop, John Coppock, Charlie Childs, Eric Washington. (*D. Allen*)

The team with supporters celebrating their success in the Village Hall. (*D. Allen*)

The cartoon that appeared in the Oxford Mail following the Nomads near victory in May 1950 against Long Hanborough. (*by courtesy of Oxford Mail & Times*)

Victory 1966.
The team that won the Oxfordshire Senior Cup against Chipping Norton at the Manor.

Back: Bill Smith (Asst. Manager), Les Smith, Keith Dolton, Dick Simmonds, Clive Wright, Brian Deard, Phil Roberts, Norman Washington (manager). Front: John Scudder, Roger Earle, Mick Washington, Norman Burnley, Mick Palmer.

'Let us make no mistake about it, this was a wonderful achievement by everyone connected with the Quarry side. Three Hellenic League teams, including the challengers for honours, Thame United and Oxford City, have fallen in the impressive victory. There are few better playing surfaces in the country at this time of year, than the Manor Ground, and the way in which Quarry's defence contained the fast moving city players, was in itself a credit to them.'

Excerpt from a letter by John Graham in the Oxford Mail.

Boys' Football

Dennis Webb remembers joining the first Barton Minors Team in 1938. It was organised by a Mr Smith and the group met in the barn at Wick Farm but played on a field in Barton Road. Before play could commence, the cows had to be moved and the cowpats collected in a wheelbarrow. Their football strips were ingeniously made by Mrs Smith out of white shirts with the collars and cuffs cut off and dyed red. The collars and cuffs were then stitched back on. They looked wonderful until it rained and the boys all turned PINK ! However the team continued and grew from strength to strength.

Barton Boys Football Teams c.1950. Adults: Den Thomas, Polly Oliver, Clifford Gurl, Pop Parsons, Plum Brown, Pedger Green, June Grain, Ernie & Louie Grain, Mr. Tull. Amongst the Players: Johnny Manger, Graham Gosling, David Rennie, — Simmonds, Sid Hood, Colin Earle, Richard Heaver, Gordon Mace.

Barton Boys Football Team in the 1950s. Players include: Plum Brown, Jimmy Duffy, Bill Hutton, Don Webb, Mr Ramsden, Ted Light, Gordon Mace, Dave Hutton, Dave Butcher (or Butler), Ernie Webb, Dave Johns, Sid Hood, 'Scottie' — , John Woodley, Pete Kemp, Colin Earle. (*M. Ramsden*)

The celebration after winning the Intermediate Cup in the early 1960s. Clockwise from top left are: Peter Wickson, Reg Trafford, Mag Page, Mrs Bover, Iris Gurl, Eve Duffy, Cliff Gurl, Ellen McLean, Dave Daffey, Harry Hudson, Brian Cox, Billy Page, Freddie Thompson, Ted Mannel, Bobby Bushnell.

Headington Quarry Cricket Team outside their Pavilion 1910. Back Row: Walter Coppock, − −, William Morris, − Goodgame. Middle Row: Cllr. George Coppock, − Trafford, George Bushnell, Tom Trafford, Mr.Bulger, Charles Coppock, − Cooper, Stephen Goodgame. Front Row: 'Smarty' Coppock, − −, George Coppock, 'Beauty' Taylor, Curate Lang, Isaac Bushnell, Tom Marshall, Frank Goodgame, boy unknown. (*I. Sheppard*)

The Headington Cricket Team originally played on the Manor Ground after the football season had finished. The condition of the pitch created difficulties for the club, which was rescued by Mr Bradley of Barton End who gave some of his land in Barton Road for the Cricket Club and a recreation ground. He is pictured with the group above in 1954. Back Row: Frank Margetts, Mick Rolf, George Kerry, Gerry Woodward, Mrs Judd (scorer), John Stevens, Ivor Judd, Joey Wilson, Reg Steele (umpire). Front Row: Jimmy Smith, George Graham, Mr Bradley (President), John Hatwell, Freddie Kimber. (*G. Kerry*)

Headington United

The 1911-12 Headington United team came second in the District League Division Two and were finalists in the City League. (*Bernard Stone*)

The foundation in 1893 of Headington United, the football club which was to play a major part in Headington life, was reported in Headington Parish magazine: '*The cricket season being over, Mr Hitchings, with his customary energy and zeal for the young men of the parish, has inaugurated a football club. A meeting for the furtherance of this object was held in the Britannia Inn on Friday evening, 27 October, and reports say that there is every prospect of getting together a good playing team. The game will be played this season under Association rules.*'

The men behind the formation of the club were the 49-year-old Vicar, Rev. Scott-Tucker, who was still an enthusiastic football player, and Dr. Hitchings. The first match was probably against the Cowley Barracks team, which Headington lost 2-1 on 25th November. The first pitch was in Headington Quarry, but until 1925 when they settled at the Manor Ground the team played at several venues including Wootten's Field in Sandy Lane, the badly drained Britannia Inn field, Quarry recreation ground and The Paddock, Manor Road.

The team played in the Junior League from 1894-7, winning the Oxford City Junior Cup in 1897-8 for the first time; bicyclists were sent off post haste to spread the good news throughout Headington, and a celebratory fireworks display was held in the evening. They won the cup again in 1898-9, in which year they were also in the final of the Oxfordshire Junior Shield.

Headington United Time Line

Above: The 1913 Headington United team. In the 1913-14 season they club won the Junior Shield final against Oxford Institute. The team members were: O. Ward, E. Britnell, J. Poole (captain), W. Anstey, A Vallis, C. Badger, W. Morris, E. McDermott, A. Phillips, E. Smith and J. Phillips. (*Bernard Stone*)

1914   Headington United won the Oxfordshire Junior Shield.
1921   They took a big step up into the Oxfordshire Senior League.
1931   Won the Oxfordshire Charity Shield for the first time and were finalists in the Oxon Senior Cup. Played their first ever F.A. Cup game against Hounslow which they lost 8-2.

Below: Headington United Senior XI in 1930-31 with the Oxfordshire Charity Shield. Back row: G. Mattock (Hon treasurer), P. Locke, A. Webb, W. Bradbury, F. Margetts, A. Douglas, A. Jacobs (Chairman). Middle row: W. Jones, J. Sawyer (Captain), Major Melvill Lee (President), J. Durran and G. Schultz, with T. Wharton and E. Coppock cross-legged in front. (*G. Coppock*)

1936   Won the Oxon Senior Cup, beating Banbury Spencer in the replay 1-0.

1938-9 Headington were the best side in Oxfordshire apart from long-time rivals Oxford City. Won the Senior League for the first time plus the Charity Cup and played in the finals of the Senior Cup.

1948   Beat Oxford City 1-0 in the Oxon Senior Cup final at the Iffley Road ground. The Oxford Mail reported 'Oxford City R.I.P.'

1949   Became semi-professional. Joined the Southern League, playing as far away as Exeter and Colchester. Manor Ground improved and crowds increased from c.3000 to over 10,000.

1952-3 Won the Southern League to become one of the top non-league clubs.

1953-4 First competitive matches against league clubs in the F.A. Cup.

1959   The team became full-time professionals.

1960   The name of the club was changed to Oxford United.

1962   Oxford United joined Division 4.

1963-4 Reached the quarter finals of the F.A. Cup — the first fourth division club to do so.

1965   Promoted to Division 3.

1968   Champions of Division 3 and promoted to Division 2.

1970   Reached the quarter finals of the League Cup (which later became the Milk Cup and the Coca-Cola Cup).

1976   Relegated to Division 3.

1981   Robert Maxwell took over the club.

1983   Scheme to merge Oxford United and Reading to form Thames Valley Royals foundered.

Below: Ken Smith scoring the only goal for Headington United which put Millwall out of the F.A. Cup in 1954. (*Les Bateman*)

Keeping the ground in good order was the job of Les Bateman who became full time grounds-man in 1949, working there until 1983 when he was 73. Here he is seen helping, from left to right: Ian White, - - , Terry Ruane and Peter Higgins to sweep the terraces. (*Les Bateman*)

1983-4 Division 3 champions, promoted to Division 2.

1984-5 Division 2 champions — only side to win in Division 3 and Division 2 in consecutive seasons.

1985-6 Won the Milk Cup 3-0 against Queen's Park Rangers, a record goal margin.

1987   Robert Maxwell became more interested in Derby County and made Kevin Maxwell Chairman of Oxford United.

1988   Controversial sale of Oxford striker Dean Saunders to Derby County.

Crowd support is always important. Here loyal supporters standing behind barriers made with lorry struts from Cowley Barracks, watch Headington play Banbury Spencer in 1952. In front from the right are Dennis Webb, Miriam, Doris and Ada Webb, Dark and Fred Biddows. (*D Webb*)

The team and staff in 1953 when they were the Southern League champions and won the Southern League Cup. Back row, left to right: Les Bateman (groundsman), — —, — —, Peart, Ron Steel, John Crighton. Frank Ramshaw, Bob Craig, Ben Duncan, — —, — —, — —, Harris. Middle row: Frank Lawrence, Harry Thompson (manager), — —, Jimmy Smith,   — —, Jack Ansell, Ernie Hudson, Harry Yates, — —, Tom Webb (physiotherapist), — —. Front: — —, — Smith, Vic Couling, Ron Coppock, — —, — —. (*G. Coppock*)

1991   Robert Maxwell drowned and Oxford United were left with financial problems.
1992   Oxford clung to their position in Division 1 by winning the last match of the
       season. Biomass took over as Chairman instead of the Maxwells.
1994   Relegation to Division 2.
1995   Robin Herd became chairman.
1996   Oxford United won promotion to Division 1 and the building of their new
       stadium at Blackbird Leys began.

The 4th round F.A. Cup match against Bolton Wanderers on 7th January 1954 which Headington lost 2-4, having previously beaten both Millwall and Stockport. (*Les Bateman*)

The team, now renamed Oxford United, were again Southern League Champions in 1962. Captain Ron Atkinson was the first player to steer his team from the Southern League up through three Football League divisions. He was captain from 1960-71 apart from 1967-8, and went on to become player-manager of Kettering. Back row: J. Shelton (trainer), P. Higgins, P. Bryan, I. White, A. Buck, J. Shuker, I. McIntosh, P. Selby, T. Jacques, T. Webb (masseur). Front: O. Medlock, G. Atkinson, A. Willey, C. Beavon, P. Knight, R. Atkinson (captain), R.S. Coppock (Chairman), A. Turner (manager), M. Kyle, T. Jones, P. Quartermain, B. Houghton, D. Denial and J. Love (*Oxford United*)

Oxford United in 1973-4 when Colin Clarke was skipper. Back row: Dave Roberts, Ray Pickett, Rodney Smithson, Roy Burton, Kevin Thomas, Peter Hatch, John Shuker, Jimmy Light. Middle row: John Fleming, Steve Flay, Derek Clarke, Hugh Curran, Nigel Cassidy, Graham Atkinson, Keith Gough, Jimmy Campbell, Nick Lowe. Front: Ken Fish (trainer), Dick Lucas, John Evanson, Geoff Bray, Gerry Summers (manager), Colin Clarke, Ken Skeen, Steve Aylott, Mick Brown (assistant manager). (*Rachel Groves*)

Above left: Robert Maxwell, Chairman from late 1981 until his death in 1991, autographing a programme with his daughter Ghislaine. He encouraged the hunt for a new stadium and brought in Jim Smith as manager. In 1982 he mooted the controversial idea of merging Oxford with Reading to form Thames Valley Royals, but it did not work. During his term as Chairman the club rose to Division One and won the Milk Cup. (*Oxford United*)

Above right: Peter Foley, an excellent goal-scorer, and Mark Higgins in the Oxford v Everton match which Oxford lost 0-1. Bicester-born Foley was associated with the club from the age of 13, becoming a full-time professional at 18. (*Oxford United*)

The crowd invading the pitch when Oxford defeated Manchester United 2-1 after two draws with them in the League Cup in 1983-4. (*Oxford United*)

The triumphant United squad mid-way through the 1986-7 season, after they had won the Milk Cup at Wembley on 20th April 1986, defeating Queen's Park Rangers 3-0 in front of a crowd of 90,396. The goals were scored by Trevor Hebberd (man of the match), Ray Houghton and Jeremy Charles. Back row: Jeremy Charles, Billy Whitehurst, Alan Judge, Gary Briggs, Steve Hardwick, Bobby McDonald, David Langan. Middle row: David Fogg (reserve team manager), Ken Fish (trainer), Kevin Brock, David Leworthy, Neil Slatter, John Dreyer, Sean Reck, Robbie Mustoe, Paul Swannack, Tony Obi, David Coates (youth development officer), Ray Graydon (assistant manager). Front: Ray Houghton, Les Phillips, Malcolm Shotton, Maurice Evans (manager), John Aldridge, Trevor Hebberd and John Trewick. (*Oxford United*)

The local derby matches with Swindon are always well supported. Here Dean Saunders shoots just wide in the Gary Briggs testimonial match in August 1987 (*Oxford United*)

Schools and Oxford Brookes University

St Andrew's School

The National School which opened as a mixed school in 1847 was sometimes known as the Field School because it stood in the middle of a field given by Charles Tawney. It was the first school in Headington apart from dame schools and the charity school founded by Catherine Mather in 1805. These small schools could no longer cater for enough children so the Church of England school was built, adapting in 1875 to run the boys' and girls' sections separately. New twin school buildings were opened in 1894, and are still in use. The Stace family exerted a strong influence as George Stace became head in 1878, retiring in favour of his son George in 1921, who in turn held the post until 1952. George Stace senior had an immediate impact, the Inspector's report for 1879 commenting: *'There has been a decided improvement both in the discipline and attainment of the boys in this school since Mr Stace took charge.'*

> The building of the Infant School at New Headington has begun. Contributions are earnestly requested by the Curate, who has made himself responsible for all expenses. £50 have been already given or promised. £250 more is required.

As the local villages expanded, a new school was built in Quarry in 1864 and an Infant School in New Headington in 1873. This extract is taken from the *Headington Parish Magazine* for May 1873.

The School Inspector came each year to examine the pupils, and funding for the following year depended on successful results. (*Headington Parish Magazine*, August 1877).

Reports of H.M's Inspector of Schools.

REV. H. A. PICKARD ON THE HEADINGTON BOYS', GIRLS',
AND INFANTS' SCHOOLS, 1877.

HEADINGTON NATIONAL SCHOOL, (OXFORD).

BOYS' SCHOOL.—MASTER, MR. YEATES.—" The Boys are now in the School formerly occupied by the Girls, which is neither so pleasant nor so commodious as the other. The Elementary Knowledge is fair, the weak points being the Dictation of the II. Standard, and the Arithmetic of the upper Standards. Grammar is imperfect throughout the School; Geography fair in the first class, moderate in the rest of the School. I attribute the deterioration in the efficiency of the School mainly to the prevalence of sickness, and to the excitement caused by the announcement of the Managers' intention to close all the Schools under their superintendence."

Grant ... ... £31 13s. 0d.

GIRLS' SCHOOL.—MISTRESS, MISS CROZIER.—" The School has increased in numbers, and the staff has been scarcely sufficient to produce very good results. The prevalence of fever has seriously impaired the efficiency of this as well as of the other Schools. It has also suffered in common with the other Schools, from the announcement that the Managers intend to close all the Schools. Notwithstanding these drawbacks, the Elementary Knowledge is fair, the Needlework very good, and half the Girls pass creditably in Grammar."

Grant ... ... £48 15s. 0d.

" T. B. Pickering has passed well. He is now qualified under both articles 60 and 79.

OLD HEADINGTON INFANTS' SCHOOL, (OXFORD).

MISTRESS, MRS. CROZIER.—" The children have been taught with care and kindness; the collective lessons are well given, and the first class pass creditably in Reading and Writing, but are rather weak in Mental Arithmetic."

Grant ... ... £36 2s. 0d.

Sepr 27th "The children were let out of school. before time on Thursday afternoon, on account of St Clements' Fair. Registers not marked. A good many late this week, they were kept in double the time they were late and some who repeated the fault were caned. Night School opens on Monday next — 3 nights per week. Miss Prmy came and took a class on Monday morning in Reading and dictation.

The log books contain much fascinating information — reasons why children were absent (following the hunt, working, no boots etc.), plus details about lessons and activities. Here is the entry from September 27th 1872, which mentions that evening classes for adults were held in the school. (*St Andrew's School*).

Some children at the Field School in 1928: Back row: — —, Peggy Miles, Arthur Neville, Gwennie Currill, — —, Peter Griffin. Middle: Freddie Edgington, — —. John Williams, Harry Thick, — —, Arthur Walker, — —. Front: Margaret Kerry, Doreen Goodwin, Edna Woodward, Daisy Mead, Margaret Folley, — —. (*Mrs Doreen Lambert, nee Goodwin*).

Class photograph c. 1933. Back row, — —, — —, — —, Sylvia Neville, — —, Eric Cann, Kathleen Stone, Margaret Taylor, 4 unknown. Middle row: — —, — —, — —, Glenys Claridge, — —, Lavinia Dennis, — —, Kathleen Welsh, , 5 unknown. Front row: — —, — —, — —, Hilda Skey, — —, Audrey Warry, 5 unknown. (*Bernard Stone*)

The first trophy won by the school football team, trained by Miss Stace, after the war. Back row: David Yates, John Murphy, Nigel Bowers, Peter 'Truck' Carter, John Vendome, Les Toms. Middle Row: Norman Woodcock, Tony Fathers, Denis Neville, Roger Chaundy, Derek Woodcock, and in front Tony Hunter and Freddie Thompson. (*Ramon Roper*)

Mrs H. Webb's classroom decorated to celebrate Queen Elizabeth II's coronation in 1953. The blond boy under the Queen's photograph is Roger Lambert, the girl second right in the back row is — Jacobs and the boys front right are Christopher Barson, — Bower and — Chaundy. (*Mrs Doreen Lambert*).

Mrs Webb taught at St Andrew's from 1941-77; here she is seen with her class in 1958. Back row: — —, — —, Clive Lambert (now Head of Bayswater School), — —, — —, — —, — —, — —, John Adams, — —, — Mullins, Mr Heath, Head Teacher. 3rd row: Valerie Smith, David Adams, — —, — —, Joss Wainwright (whose father used to be Head of Cheney School), — —, Michael Berry, Ann -, — —, Susan Liberman, — —. 2nd row: — —, — —, — —, Linda Abstone, Mary Church, rest unknown. Front row: unknown. (*Mrs H. Webb*)

Headington Quarry Church of England School

List of Object Lessons for
1893 – 1894.

Division I Elephant An orange   The Baker   Spring
            Sheep   Bells   The Blacksmith Summer
            Frog   Cotton   The Brickmaker Autumn
            Cow   Candles   Soldiers   Winter
            Wolf   A ship   Sailors   Water
            Bee   Money   The Shoemaker Ice
            Goat   Sugar
            Snail   Pictures
            Camel   A lighthouse

Division II The cow, The cat, The dog, The sheep,
             Bells, An orange, Pictures, A railway
             station, The gardener, The baker
                 Form and Colour for both classes.

                    Varied Occupations
Division   I   II   III
           Embroidery. Wool Flowers. Fraying.
           Mat weaving. Cork Work.   Stick Laying.
           Straw and.   Wool Balls.   Bead Threading.
           paper Threading.

Headington Quarry National School opened in 1864. The log book entry for 1893 shows some of the 'object' lessons in which the children were taught about particular topics, with little or no visual aids apart from drawings on the blackboard. (*Headington Quarry School*)

April 4th   Diocesan Inspector's Report.

        "Examined March 31. 1898
The infants answered brightly and the repetition throughout
the school was excellent both in quantity and in quality.
The school generally is in a satisfactory and promising
condition as regards religious Knowledge.
     Albert Cooper, Richard Collins, Phyllis Durham, Thomas Jones,
George Vallis, Mary Trafford deserve mention.
                    R. Hutchison Dioc. Insp."
                 true copy C. F. H. Johnston
                            Manager.

Church of England Schools were visited each year by the Diocesan Inspector — this glowing report dates from 1898. (*Headington Quarry School*)

Children outside Quarry School c. 1907-8. Ada Webb (nee Washington) is seated second left in the second row. Her father William Washington was the Fool for the Quarry Morris Men. (*Ada Washington*)

Some Quarry schoolchildren dressed up as 'Nursery Rhymes' c.1929. (*Annie Hatwell*)

Headington Council School, Margaret Road

Headington Council School opened in 1908, catering for 150 infants and 220 children. Note the state of Margaret Road. The schools have now been renamed Windmill First School and Headington Middle School. (*Jill Slaymaker*)

Headington Infants in 1913, with teacher Mabel Nutt. Back row, left to right: Charles and Elsie Higginson, Reggie Barton, − Gardiner, Willie Wharton, Percy Yeatman and Jack Toms. Centre: Georgie Coppock, Ronald Hathaway, − Neville, − −, Jim Newman, Cissy Savins, Olive Blackwell, − −, Rose Cole and Ada Morris. Front: Tom Cann, Edith Soames, Georgie Thrustle, Stanley Allmond, Betty Taylor, Mary Cann, Arthur Cousins, Margaret Eagleton, Jimmy Taylor and Fred Spring. (*M.A.Coppock*)

A scene from *The Wedding of the Painted Doll* performed at the Infants' School Christmas concert c1930. The bride is Hazel Hall, the groom Charles Hall and in the front row are — —, Rowland Morris — —, Harold Jeffs. (*Joyce Allen, nee Morris*)

The Infants' Christmas pantomime c.1931. Joyce Morris is in the front row, third from right. (*Joyce Allen*)

A fancy dress competition at the school in 1949. Bernard Stone, third from the left, is wearing a costume made from wartime blackout material depicting the nursery rhyme *Oranges and Lemons.* (*Bernard Stone*)

The Senior School Athletics team that won the County Cup in 1938. Back, left to right, Joyce Morris, ? Freda Spiers, − −, ? Susan Beauchamp. Front: − −, Betty Bunyan, Jean Hosier, − Allsop, Joan Wright and ? Eunice Bradbury. (*Joyce Allen*).

An adult fitness class at the school, c.1940s, with Joyce Morris second from left, Jean Fairweather (nee Clark) on her right.   (*Joyce Allen*)

School camping holiday in Guernsey, 1955. Left to right: Derek Bird, Michael Grace, Peter Smith, Tim Church and in front is the son of Mr Goodall, the teacher accompanying the group. (*Bernard Stone*)

Barton Infants' School

The school opened in 1951 and is now renamed Barton Village First School. Here Miss Hubble and her staff are seen at the opening of the swimming pool in 1958. (*Ann Every*)

Barton Junior School

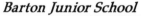

This opened in 1949 and is now known as Bernwood First School. Here a group of schoolchildren are seen on a trip to Wytham church in 1953. The group includes Jill Bennett, Peter Every, Keith Webb, Maureen Jenkins, Tony James, Keith White, Christopher Hopkins, Dave Pearson, Christine Thomas, Sheila Boilteaux, Linda Evans, Valerie King, Maureen Wiggins, Michael Clare, Bill Simonds, Keith King, Roy Carter, Terry Twine, Clifford Lambourne, Richard Heaver, Graham Sheppard, Alan Davies and Mr Andrews. (*R. Heaver*)

Wood Farm School

The first schools built on this site in Titup Hall Drive in 1956 were Wood Farm Infants, for children aged 5-7 and Wood Farm Juniors for 7-11 year olds which were housed in what are now known respectively as the Joan Lawrence and Mary Bews buildings. With reorganisation in 1974 both changed to become Shotover Way and Forresters First Schools, amalgamating in 1980 to become Wood Farm School. In 1983 the Slade Nursery transferred from its original site on the Slade to the Joan Lawrence Building and in the mid 1980s, Forresters Playgroup occupied the temporary classroom. The Community Centre was created by extending the office accommodation in the Mary Bews Building in 1991.

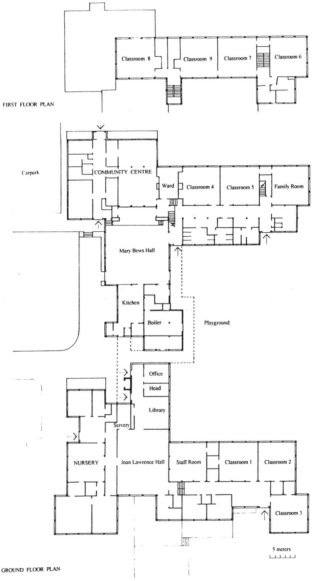

Ground plan of the school by the Facilities Planning Group. (*H.A. Shatford*)

Right: Staff gathered together at the retirement of Mrs Muriel Henderson, Head of Shotover Way First School, in 1976, after 13 years as head. The school presented her with a travelling alarm clock, and organised a surprise concert. From left to right are Jeannette Dallimore, Mary Yoshimoto, Margaret Chambers, Joan Blake, Muriel Henderson, Iris Matthews, Jean Ellis, Mary Morrison, Kathleen Bownas and Cynthia Dunford. (*Margaret Chambers*)

Children at Wood Farm Infants' School performing a Nativity Play in 1964. (*Margaret Chambers*)

Bayswater School

Staff and students in 1955, back row: deputy head Richard Caistor, Headmaster Kingsley Gallop and Mr Defalla with pupils — —. Rose —, Janet Allsworth, Myra Palmery, Maureen Segar, Pat Bucket, Diane -, and in front Wally Garner, Brian Smith and Malcolm Every. (*M. Every*)

Bayswater Secondary Modern School opened in September 1953, drawing pupils mainly from the rapidly expanding Barton. Academic standards rose and sporting excellence was nurtured, several pupils representing Oxford city in sports. Between 1973-5 Bayswater was converted to a middle school. Pupils came from a larger catchment area including Headington. Activities ranged from a Science Club and Chess Club to painting the underpass and camping at Hillend.

School outing to the Oxfordshire Show c.1960, showing from the back: Pete Lannigan, Dougie Smith, centre Michael Davis and Henry (Chalkie) White and front, Ronnie Lee. (*M. Every*)

The old school crest embroidered on a house banner. (*Bayswater Middle School*)

The school staff in September 1978. Back row: Mr Wilson (P.E., 1st year team), Mr Keith Ponsford (P.E., then head of 4th year, later deputy head at Marston), Mr Piper (geography and English), Mr Roper (caretaker), Mr Pemberton (science technician). 3rd row: Mr Brown (history, 2nd year head), Mr Parker (mathematics), Mrs Beith (1st year teacher), Mr Fisher (science), Miss Harwood (P.E.), Mrs Capel (2nd year team teacher). 2nd row: Mrs Cox (art), Mrs Brees (French, later senior mistress), Mrs Blunt (needlework), Mrs Webb (school secretary), Miss Edwards (1st year teacher), Mrs Potter (2nd year teacher), Miss Collicott (French). Front row: Mrs Harvey (school secretary), Mr Lander (woodwork, 4th year team leader), Mrs Thomas (domestic science), Mr Awde (English), Mr Whittingham (Head teacher), Mr Munday (deputy head), Mrs Kirkpatrick (senior mistress), Miss Lewis (music), Miss Gilchrist (2nd year head). (*David Munday*)

Landform in Stone, the sculpture in the school grounds, was created by Peter Fink in 1984, sponsored by the Arts Council of Great Britain, the Gulbenkian Foundation and Rank Xerox. (*Adrian Shatford*)

Private Schools
Miss Edney's School

Miss Edney, the aunt of tailor Alan Edney, ran a small school for young children at 48 Old High Street. Kathleen Eastes (nee Stone) remembers: *'I started at the age of five in 1929... The two Miss Edneys were a very good team, one teaching and the other doing the cooking and domesticated jobs. The hunt used to meet on the Black Boy forecourt, and it was with great excitement that we were allowed to stand on our chairs and watch the red-coated huntsmen with the hounds ... Unfortunately after a year the school had to close due to the ill-health of one of the sisters.'*

Top: 48 Old High Street.

Left: Kathleen Harris, nee Stoppes, is one of the daisies dressed up for a function at Miss Edney's school c 1927-8. (*Kathleen Harris*)

Miss Steff's School

Left: Miss Steff kept a kinder-garten school in a corrugated iron hut at 41 Church Street (now St Andrew's Road) from the 1880s until she retired aged 72 in 1931.In 1932 Mrs E.C. Steenbuck took over the school, although Miss Steff still lived at the house. By 1935 Miss Ward had taken over, but the school closed by 1939. (*Adrian Shatford*)

St Anne's School

Mrs Steenbuck ran St Anne's School at 8 St Anne's Road from 1935-45 for about 30 children aged between 5-14.

Right: Joyce Webb dressed as a fairy at the school Christmas Concert. (*Joyce Webb*)

Cheney School

A view of Cheney School and below the school coat of arms.

Cheney School has a long and distinguished history, being an amalgamation in 1972 of the Junior part of the Secondary Technical School (which had formed part of the School of Art since 1870, moving up from its last home in St Ebbes to Cheney Lane in 1955), and Cheney Girls' School (formerly Central School) which moved from New Inn Hall Street to a site next to Cheney in 1959.

Arnold Wainwright was headmaster from 1937-71. During his tenure the school changed from being a junior branch of the Technical College to a selective Technical School, with the emphasis changing from vocational work to concentration on G.C.E. examinations. The prospectus read: *'The School aims at providing a type of Secondary Education suited to abler children who have . . . a marked practical aptitude . . . Most of the pupils on leaving the School will be qualified to proceed to full-time . . . advanced courses in technology, art or commerce, with a view to ultimately fitting themselves for responsible technical appointments in industry or commerce, as teachers of special subjects in various types of schools, for careers such as nursing, or for employment as mastercraftsmen and women.'* (*Cheney School*)

Work in progress in the art room of Cheney Girls' School in 1967. (*Cheney School*)

Sport plays an important part in school life — the Cheney Girls' School Magazine for 1965 reported increased enthusiasm for tennis: *'There is a full fixture list which includes two matches against boys' schools and a mixed match in which we combine with Cheney Boys.'* In the 1965 team were (back row): Marilyn Brackley, Linda Jeffs, Jennifer Elliott, Linda Maddan, Janice Hall and Deborah Merry; (front row): Susan Hale, Mary Dodman. Stephanie Harris, Anne Morrison and Gillian Clark. (*Cheney School*)

The 1967 Second XI football team, (back row) D. Sweeney, P. Cox, M. Lowen, P. Giles, I. Stone, M. Chandler, G. Peaper, J. Skipp, (front row): J. Baker, J. Kent, R. Peterson and A. Wright, played the staff, and an 'unbiased' teacher reported in the school magazine:

' . . . the Staff employed tactics more suited to Oxford United and the fact that Mr Hudson was carried off after being chopped down by the entire half-back line was purely accidental. The School did 99% of the attacking and some good goalkeeping by Brian Long . . . and some biased refereeing kept the School's total down to one goal . . . The Staff managed to grab four goals but we believe this was only because . . . the Cheney School team were signing autographs for the large crowd...' (Cheney School)

The first pupils to achieve Duke of Edinburgh gold awards, (those marked with a ★ from Cheney School), at Oxford Station in December 1961. Back row: Bernard Blackwell★, Bernard Stone★, Richard Booth★, Kenneth Guy, Mr P. L. Bickerton (who ran the scheme), Alan Giles, John Gardner. Front row: Graham McKenzie, − −, Brian Garland★, − − and David Smith. (*Bernard Stone*)

Headington School

Above left: Miss MacGregor became the first headmistress of Headington School when it opened in 1915, leaving to marry two years later. (*Headington School*)

Above centre: Miss Porcher, her successor, steered the school through many changes such as the purchase of Brookside (renamed Napier House when the original Napier was sold in 1931) and Davenport House in 1920. Most importantly, the new school buildings were opened on 21st June 1930 by H.R.H. Princess Mary, who commented: *'This will ever be to me a most memorable day, in which I have first of all received a degree from the University and secondly opened these very beautiful school buildings.'* (*Headington School*)

Above right: Miss Moller who became headmistress in 1934, helped the war effort by hosting evacuees from Francis Holland School, while Davenport House was requisitioned as a maternity hospital. She retired in 1959. (*Headington School*)

Aerial view of the school.

Girls playing hockey, the principal sport at the school, in 1948. (*Headington School*)

H.R.H. Princess Mary, the Princess Royal, returned to the school in 1963 to open two new boarding houses and start the new tower clock. (*Headington School*)

Girls studying in the science laboratory in 1948. (*Headington School*)

Oxford Brookes University

An aerial view of the Brookes site on Headington Hill. (*Oxford Brookes University*)

Brookes originated in 1865 in the Oxford School of Art, run in the Taylor Institution, St Giles. A School of Science was incorporated into it in 1870. The School moved to St Ebbes, but rapidly ran out of space. John Brookes was appointed Vice Principal in 1928, becoming Principal of the renamed Schools of Technology, Art and Commerce in 1934. The Headington Hill site was purchased in 1949, but it was not until 1954 that the foundation stone for the new buildings for the College of Technology, Art and Commerce was laid by former pupil Lord Nuffield. Having been a Polytechnic since 1970 it was raised to the status of a university and renamed after its former Principal John Brookes in 1992 with the first Chancellor, appointed in 1994, being Helena Kennedy QC. The University now uses Headington Hill Hall in addition to the main site.

John Brookes, O.B.E., whose wisdom, foresight and good management influenced the development of the College, seen on his 80th birthday. He was himself an expert craftsman in stone and silver. (*Oxford Brookes University*)

H.R.H. Prince Philip, Duke of Edinburgh, opened the new college buildings in 1963. To his left is the Director Brian Lloyd, to his right Professor Holcroft, chairman of the Governors, and to the left behind the Duke is Detective Sergeant Magson of Oxford City Police. (*Oxford Brookes University*)

A tutorial in the Department of Architecture. Architecture was first added to the curriculum in 1929. (*Oxford Brookes University*)

A group of students indulging in a game of croquet in the grounds, c.1960s. At that time the top two floors of the building behind them housed the Department of Architecture, the bottom two art and the pottery department was on the ground floor. The building to the right was the administrative block. (*Oxford Brookes University*)

Headington Businesses

Mattock's Nurseries

Market gardening used to be an important occupation in Headington, and the most famous firm is that of Mattock's. John Mattock was born in Steeple Ashton near Bath and was sent off on a carrier's cart at the age of 14 to be apprenticed as a gardener. He came to Oxford in the early 1870s to work for the Davenports of Headington Hill. He gradually began to buy land in Headington and had set up his own business by 1875; he was described in the Oxford City & Suburban Directory for that year as a tea dealer, gardener and florist. He became a major supplier of fruit, vegetables and plants to the Oxford colleges.

John Mattock (1827-1913) with his wife Harriet (born c 1829), whom he had met while they were both in service, and their young son John II, born in 1863, taken c.1865. (*Mark Mattock*)

Eighty-eight Windmill Road built by the Mattocks c.1890 when John Mattock moved from Bath Buildings (behind William Street — now Wilberforce Street New Headington), with a greenhouse beside it. His nursery gardens stretched behind the house and towards Old Road. (*Mark Mattock*)

Telegraphic Address:—"Mattock, Headington, Oxford."

Season 1896-1897.

Descriptive Catalogue
OF
ROSES,

CULTIVATED FOR SALE
BY
JOHN MATTOCK,
Nurseryman and Florist,

NEW HEADINGTON, OXFORD,
(Entrance to the Nursery from Wind Mill Lane,)
AND
73 & 74, THE MARKET, OXFORD.

INSPECTION INVITED.

John Mattock began to specialise in roses — at the Headington Horticultural and Poultry Show in September 1892 he was praised for his entry: *'One very noticeable collection was a dozen blooms of "Mrs John Laing", a hybrid perpetual, soft pink in colour, very large and of fine form. These came from Mr. John Mattock, who also put up, not for competition, thirty-six varieties of roses, and a dozen bunches of button-hole roses . . .'* In 1896 he was awarded 57 prizes for his roses at shows as diverse as Oxford, Bath, Reading, Ealing, Crystal Palace, Halifax, Taunton and Trowbridge, to mention a few. By the early 1920s his son John II was exhibiting in Glasgow and Belfast, and more recently the firm have won five consecutive gold medals at the Royal Horticultural Society's show at Chelsea. In 1975, to celebrate the first hundred years of the firm, a new red rose, Centurion, was created.

Mattock's Catalogue, 1896-7 (*Mark Mattock*).

Mattocks has always been a family business. Here John Mattock I is show with his son John R. (1863-1937), who ran his own business as a florist from 1894-99 at Summerville House, Highfield, then worked with his father. John II's brother William was a market gardener at Barton. John II's son John W (1898-1973) followed in the family tradition. The firm had shops at 73 and 74 Oxford Market run by John I's daughters Harriet Rose and Amelia. John R. married Elizabeth Drake, mistress of St Andrew's Girls' School from 1884-92, then moved into 90 Windmill Road, built at a cost of £500. She was highly regarded and the school managers presented her with a plated tea service as a wedding present, declaring that: *'We cannot speak too highly of the conscientious way in which she has discharged her duties, and of the valuable influence she has exerted over her scholars.'* Excerpt from Headington Parish Magazine, June 1892. (*Mark Mattock*)

The staff of Mattock's c1880 with William Mattock second left, back row in a bowler hat, his brothers George (probably back row second from right) and John R (*back right*), with the bearded foreman seated in the centre. The firm stayed in Headington until the council compulsorily purchased their land for building in the 1960s, when they moved to Nuneham Courtenay. Headington still boasts Wests' nursery in Windmill Road, which has been at the same premises at least since 1876. (*Mark Mattock*)

The rose budding staff in 1906 with John R Mattock and his young son John W. in the centre. The lads grafted varieties of rose buds to grow on briar stock. According to family tradition, most of the boys depicted here joined the Oxford and Bucks Light Infantry to fight in the First World War and were killed by the same shell. (*Mark Mattock*)

Dring's Carriers and Coach Company

Alfred Dring outside his premises in Windmill Road with his wife Edith holding baby Edith (Edie) and Alfred's parents, taken in 1904. (*Peter Dring*)

Alfred Dring (c1880-1946) came to Headington at the age of 14 in 1894 and set up a carriers' business based in Windmill Road c.1902, when the only other Headington carrier was George Jacob, both going to Oxford twice daily. In 1902 he married Edith Honey, a laundress from Highfield.

Alfred Dring gradually built up his business — in 1910 he introduced the Rocket horse-bus service between Headington and Oxford. Because of the steepness of Headington Hill he stabled additional horses at the bottom of the hill.

The Dring family at the rear of the premises with two of their horses. (*Peter Dring*)

Above left: Alfred Dring, photographed in the early 20th century. Above centre: Alfred and Edith Dring's children Edie (born in 1904) and Alfred Charles (born c 1908) in their back garden. Above right: Walter Edward Dring, Alfred's second son, born c. 1916. Both boys joined the family firm when they left school. (*Peter Dring*)

Alfred Dring hired out carriages for weddings and funerals. His daughter Edie can be seen leaning out of the window outside the Windmill Road premises c. 1908. (*Peter Dring*)

Passengers setting off on an outing to the seaside — note the little girl in a beret with her bucket and spade. Alfred Charlesworth, the driver, stands in a peaked cap at the back. (*Sylvia Dring*)

Dring's coaches waiting in New High Street in the 1930s. The one on the left is an older soft-topped version. They have the firm's famous Oxford Blue logo. Alfred Dring stands third from the left in the group of drivers. Alfred died in 1947, but his sons carried on the firm until the early 1960s. (*Sylvia Dring*)

ALFRED DRING,

CARRIER, Headington to Oxford.

Leaves "Chequers," High Street, and "New Inn," Daily.

Open and Closed Carriages for Hire.   Special Journeys Arranged.

A Conveyance called "The Rocket,"

WILL RUN DAILY, HEADINGTON TO CARFAX.

TIMES OF STARTING.		RETURNING.
10.30 a.m.		12.30 p.m.
2.30 p.m.		4.30 ,,
5.30 ,,		6.30 ,,
8 ,,	Saturdays only	8.30 ,,

Luggage and Parcels Conveyed to all parts Daily.

Dring advertising card for 'The Rocket' c1910 (*Sylvia Dring*)

Dring advertising card for Oxford Blue Coaches — the one illustrated has a soft top which rolls back. Later Crappers used a blue livery for their coaches, so Dring's changed to cream and red. (*Sylvia Dring*)

Dring's letter heading, printed in magenta and maroon, showing some of the excursions offered, c1950s (*Peter Dring*)

Griffi
Garag

Mr Griffin began as a carrier, changing to a garage business c. 1939. Here his horse and cart are seen in Cornmarket Street during the First World War. Arthur Jacob drove the horse and cart for Mr Griffin at this time. After the war he bought this part of the business and started A.G. Jacob and Sons, the removal firm which still operates from Windmill Road. (*Bernard Stone*)

Right: Griffin's advertisement from Kelly's Directory in the 1940s. (*Reed Information Systems*)

Below: Griffin's Garage at 103 London Road. Reginald Ernest Griffin is sitting in the lorry and Charles 'Son' Costar stands by the petrol pump. In 1954 it was renamed Central Garage and moved to 17A Old High Street, finally closing c1972. (*Bernard Stone*)

Central   Garage,   Headington,   Oxford

Phone: OXFORD **6895**

R. E. GRIFFIN

Lock~ups

Car Sales, Exchanges.   DEFERRED TERMS

Motor Cars for Hire.   Petrol, Oils, Dunlop Tyres

Berry Family

The Berrys were a large family; the sons William and Jim ran the bakery in Old Headington from Mathers Farm until the first World War, then from Stone House next door. Jim had been to university and later became Head Postmaster in Cambridge. Harry Berry of Lower Farm ran the butcher's shop at the church end of Old High Street and his sisters Alice and Muriel worked in the shop. Mary Berry (Polly), John R. Mattock's second wife, was run over and killed in the Cowley Road in her 90s.

William Berry, a prominent local businessman, seen in his regalia as Sheriff of Oxford in 1940. (*J. Stooke*)

The Berry family photographed after the funeral of their mother, Sarah Ann Berry in January 1926. Back row: left to right, (numbered to show their order of age): Mildred (10), Josephine (11), Jim (12), Edith (8), Mary (5), Harry (2) and Florence (9). Front Row: Fanny (6), Liz (4), William (1), Sally (3) and Alice (7). (*J. Stooke*)

Customs and Folklore

Customs formed part of the country calendar which gave people a sense of how time was passing in the days before television and other media. At New Year people performed a candle dance, jumping over a lighted candle — if it went out during the dance it was a bad omen. In Old Headington a Marsh and Bush revel was held on Whitsunday until the 18th century, at which the people indulged in rural sports and games and danced to tunes played by gypsy fiddlers. Orlando Jewitt, the engraver, recorded another Whitsun custom, electing a Mock Mayor of Old Headington, in *The Antiquary*, February 1910, where the mayor was:

'chaired on men's shoulders, in a bower of evergreens, round its confines on the Wednesday of Whitsun week. This gentleman was generally in a state of delightful inebriety, having imbibed before setting out "not wisely but too well", as had his bearers, and a call being made at each public house (some three in number), and fresh potations indulged in, it may easily be imagined that towards the end of their perambulation most of the performers were more than slightly obfuscated, indeed at times it resulted in a broken limb for the unfortunate recipient of mayoral honours.'

On Guy Fawkes Day until the mid 19th century boys made guys, who according to Orlando Jewitt *'often took the form of some objectionable and unpopular person, for I remember a deservedly obnoxious publican being burnt in effigy in front of his house.'*
The boys had a menacing song they sang while collecting fuel for their bonfire:

> *Remember, remember, the Fifth of November,*
> *Bonfire Night.*
> *We want a faggot to make it alight.*
> *Hatchets and Duckets,*
> *Beetles and wedges,*
> *If you don't give us some,*
> *We'll pull your old hedges.*
> *If you won't give us one, we'll take two*
> *The better for us and the worse for you."*

Percy Manning, *Folklore*, volume 14, 1903

On Christmas Day Quarry folk used to look through their apple trees at noon to see whether they could see the sun shining through: if it did they knew they would have a good crop the following autumn.

May Day

In Headington on May morning children made flower-decked garlands on sticks based round hoops and paraded from house to house in groups of four: two girls dressed in their best white frocks with long sashes, ribbons and flower-decorated caps carried each garland, followed by a boy and girl dressed as Lord and Lady, linked by a white handkerchief, the Lady carrying a large purse, singing:

> 'Gentlemen and ladies,
> We wish you a happy May,
> We have come to shew you a garland,
> Because it is May day.'

One of the bearers requested: 'Please to handsel the lord and lady's purse.' The Lord doffed his cap in thanks for the money and kissed the Lady.

Percy Manning recorded another Headington May song (*MS Top Oxon d. 199*, Bodleian Library):

> Good morning, mistress and masters,
> I wish you a happy May,
> I am come to shew my garland,
> Because it is May Day.
> A bunch of May I have brought you,
> And at your door I stand;

> It is but a bit and I can't spare it,
> 'Tis the work of my lord's hand.
> And now I have sung my short little song,
> No longer can I stay.
> May God bless you all, both great & small,
> And give you a very happy May.'

The children of Headington Quarry School celebrating May Day in 1927, the girls dressed in their best white dresses with ribbons, and several hoop garlands. Dorothy Auger was the May Queen. (*Russell Auger*)

Around the turn of the century the Quarry children started out with their garlands at about 5.45am, going from door to door and wishing the householder *"Good morning, master and mistress . . ."* and hoping for a contribution. The children often carried garlands on sticks with little dolls hanging from them.

May Day celebrations at Headington Quarry School in 1925. May Queen Hilda Washington stands in the centre, with Ellen Hare to her left and Cathy Cooper to her right with Liz Coppock and Cicely Kimber in front. The Queen was chosen by putting all the girls' names into a hat and drawing one out. (*Headington Morris Men's Scrapbook*)

Annie Hatwell was May Queen at Quarry School in 1933. Here she is shown carrying her basket of flowers and with her attendants. (*Annie Hatwell*)

Headington Quarry Morris Men

Headington Quarry morris men and friends outside the Chequers c. 1876, thought to be the oldest surviving photograph of them. The morris men are, seated from left to right: Musician Francis Cummings, William Kimber senior (the foreman of the side until 1887), James Hedges, John Horwood, Robert Cooper, the Fool John Haynes, unknown man with collecting box, with Joseph and Robert Trafford in front. (*OPA*)

The history of the Quarry morris men goes back at least to the early 19th century if not before and the team was active throughout most of the century until 1887, then declined for a decade until the folklorist Percy Manning persuaded them to dance again for him, taught by James Hedges and Thomas Horwood. The photograph above was used to reconstruct correct costumes. The dancers were drawn from a variety of Quarry occupations:

Robert Cooper	(born 1850)	stone pit labourer
Francis Cummings	(born c1798)	shoemaker
John Haynes	(born c1873)	carter and labourer
James Hedges	(born 1852)	labourer
John Horwood	(born 1852)	labourer and brickmaker
William Kimber	(born 1848)	carter, then labourer and bricklayer
Joseph Trafford	(born 1838)	brickmaker
Robert Trafford	(born 1845)	plough boy, mason's labourer, waller and mason

Mark Cox playing the fiddle as the men perform a stick dance in 1899, possibly Bean Setting which imitates dibbing a hole with a stick and planting beans, watched by the Fool, 'Sip' Washington. (*OPA*)

In the 19th century the team danced throughout Whitsun week: in Oxford on Monday, returning to the Havelock Lodge of Oddfellows' Feast at the Britannia; on Tuesday they went to church, danced at two feasts round Quarry, ending with country dancing. They rested on Wednesday then spent the rest of the week touring local villages.

The morris men outside the Chequers, June 26th 1899, top row: 3rd and 4th from left: John Horwood and 'Gran' Hedges. Middle row, 3rd, 5th and 6th from left William 'Sip' Washington, fiddler Mark Cox and Charles 'Mac' Massey. Seated, front row: Mrs John Cooper, George 'Spuggle' Coppock, William 'Mac' Massey, George 'Cobby' Coppock and Thomas 'Russian' Jones. (*OPA*)

William Kimber playing the concertina for the team in 1928. The dancers are, from left to right: — —, Arthur Kimber, 'Captain' Parsons, Charlie Jones, Jim Phillips, Fred Kimber and Percy Bateman. (*Morris Dancers' Scrapbook*). Seeing the Quarry men dance inspired Cecil Sharp to investigate morris dancing: the team set out on Boxing Day 1899 during a hard winter when the men, who worked in building trades, had not worked for three weeks. They danced at Sandfield Cottage, London Road, photograph of plaque below (*H. A. Shatford*), where Sharp was staying with his mother-in-law, the owner Mrs Burch. Sharp was fascinated and noted down tunes. Later Kimber was teaching morris dancing to girls at Mary Neal's Esperance Club in London when he met Sharp again and they co-operated for the next 24 years. Kimber was presented with the English Folk Song and Dance Society's Gold Badge in 1961. He died on Boxing Day 1961 in his 90th year and is buried in Quarry churchyard. (*H. A. Shatford*)

HERE ON BOXING DAY 1899 CECIL SHARP FIRST HEARD WILLIAM KIMBER PLAY THE HEADINGTON QUARRY MORRIS DANCE TUNES.

Above: Dancing on Shotover Mound in 1955 - left row, front to back: Geoff Hall, Jack Morris and Terry Phipps, right row, Mervyn Cox, Peter Craft and John Graham. Many boys were taught dancing at Margaret Road School by Mrs Elsie Caistor, who helped to keep the tradition alive. (Morris Dancers' Scrapbook)

The men danced to about 24 tunes - their 1899 programme included:

Handkerchief dances	Stick dances
Blue Eyed Stranger	*Constant Billy*
Country Gardens	*Raikes of Marlow*
How do-e-do Sir	*Bean Setting*
Haste to the Wedding	*Rodney*
Trunk Oles	*Draw back*

The White Rose, the anthem of the Quarry Morris Men. (*recorded by John Graham*)

The team is much in demand to provide a ceremonial arch for weddings.

The men use their sticks to make the arch at the wedding of Sylvia Gilland (nee Spokes) and John Graham at the Oxford Registry Office on November 20th, 1970. On the left of the arch are Francis Parsons, Bob Turrell, Terry Phillips. – –, and on the right: Bob Grant, Peter Scudder and Eddie Whitehouse. (*Morris Dancers' Scrapbook*)

The team at the wedding of Beryl Pitt and John Warland at St Andrew's Church, Headington in 1950. Left to right: Arthur Kimber, Charlie Jones, Jim Phillips, Beryl Pitt and John Warland, Harry and William Kimber. (*Morris Dancers' Scrapbook*)

Quarry dancers outside the White Horse, London Road, c1950s.

One of the morris songs is Roasted Woman:
Take an Old Woman and Roast Her
And Baste Her Well with Cheese
Taker out on a Cold Winter night
I am sure the Lady Would Freeze.

Take her out the Next Morning
Put her in a bundle of Straw
Then set Fire to the Bottom
I am Sure the Old Lady Would Thaw.

Jim Phillips, a member of the Quarry morris team, when he was Squire of the Morris Ring, in Bury Knowle Park, September 1959, when Quarry hosted the Ring meeting. (*Morris Dancers' Scrapbook*).

The team dance each year on Spring Bank Holiday Monday in William Kimber Crescent, named in honour of their musician, and are seen here in 1967. Left row: front to back, Terry Phipps, Bob Grant and Peter Scudder, right Barry Jones, Bob Turrell and Tony Morris. (*Morris Dancers' Scrapbook*)

The team dancing at Headington Quarry School Fete in 1974: musician John Graham, left row, front to back Francis Parsons, Bob Grant and Peter Davies, right Roger Phillips, Bob Turrell and Peter Scudder. (*Morris Dancers' Scrapbook*)

Headington Mummers

Above and below: The Quarry Mummers in 1901 in the meeting place of Court Napoleon 6829 of the Order of Foresters in the Chequers, which was also the HQ of the morris, photographed by E.J.Binney, top one described as 'King George dead. Turkish knight on the left'. (*Morris Dancers' Scrapbook*)

Two versions of the play are known from this date, one featuring King George, Turkey Snipe, Doctor Brown, Almond Nick and Jolly Jack, and the other, taught to William Kimber by his father, had Father Christmas as master of ceremonies, while the Prussian King fought the Duke of Cumberland, other characters were the Doctor, Jack Finney and a fiddler. Traditional mumming died out in 1914.

Bob Turrell as Jack Finney, Boxing Day 1967.

The current version of the play was recorded from a mummer by Quarry W.I., performed by them and published in their *'History of Headington Quarry and Shotover'* (1933).

It features Father Christmas, King George, the Turkey Snite (a corruption of 'Turkish Knight'), Beelzebub, The Doctor, Jack Finney and a fiddler. It has been performed by several different groups and actors are now drawn from the morris dancers. Much of the original text is lost so they *ad lib.* They start at the Crown and Thistle at about 11am on Boxing day, touring from pub to pub, accompanied by hand bell ringers.

Musician John Graham and Robin Ainly as Father Christmas, 1967.

Below right: ''In comes I . . .' Robin Ainly as Father Christmas, 1967. (*Morris Dancers' Scrapbook*)

The mummers in 1974, left to right: Tony Morris, Barry Jones (King George), Mall Price (Father Christmas), Francis Parsons, Roger Phillips, Bob Turrell in top hat as Jack Finney, Roy Parsons (Beelzebub), Bob Grant (Turkish Knight), Peter Scudder and Robin Ainly (Big Head). (*Morris Dancers' Scrapbook*).

Father Christmas enters, '... *Welcome, or welcome not*...'
The hero, King George, '*a man of courage bold*', enters, to be challenged by the Turkey Snite, who claims he has '*come all the way from Tyrkey-land to fight.*' Both lay claim to the King of Egypt's daughter (who does not appear in the play). They fight, King George is wounded to the heart and on comes the Doctor, who can cure:

> '*All sorts of diseases, such as the hipsy, the pipsy and the gout,*
> *Pains within and pains without.*
> *If the devil's in him, I'll fetch him out.*
> *A touch on the heart and a touch on the knee,*
> *Rise up, King George and follow me.*'

He is followed by Beelzebub, carrying a club and a can :

> '*Don't you think I am a funny old man.*'

Next comes Jack Finney, who demands to be called Mr Finney, and finally the Fiddler. The play is now preceded by handbell ringing and followed by sword dancing, traditionally done in the north of England, but taught to the Quarry men by Dr Robin Parsons who was affiliated to Quarry Morris in 1953 while he trained at the Radcliffe, and then by Bob Clarkson, a Geordie stationed at Cowley Barracks, who taught the men new figures from a different sword dance tradition.

The Shotover Giant

The sand pit at Shotover showing some of the 'giant's marbles'. (*H. A. Shatford*)

Old tales suggest that the hill was originally called Shotover because a man named Lears Hill who lived at Lye Hill, Wheatley, shot arrows over the hill to his friend Harry Bear's house in Headington Quarry to let him know he wanted to talk to him or that Harry used to shoot over to Littleworth. One of the fossils found on Shotover was known as Harry Bear's beard. Oliver Cromwell is said to have shot his musket over Shotover.

Another version was that it was a giant who shot the arrow over the hill. The last remaining legend of the Shotover Giant is preserved by the Giant's marbles, the local name for the rounded stones scattered around Shotover which he is said to have hurled. In the 17th century, according to the antiquary John Aubrey, the figure of a giant was carved on the side of the hill: '*on Shotover Hill was heretofore (not long before the Civil Wars, in the memory of man) the effigies of a Giant, cutt in ye earth as the White horse by Ashbury-parke.*' Sadly there are no known illustrations to show what it looked like, but it may have had a bow or staff in its hand. No traces have ever been found, and even its location is now lost. A 60 foot long bank (possibly a Neolithic long barrow) which stood on Shotover Plain until it was ploughed down by tanks during the Second World War, was nicknamed the Giant's Grave, and in unsupported tradition was also said to have been a mass grave for civil war victims. Thomas Gillet wrote a long poem about the mighty giant Bullingdon who fought for the 'Britons' against the Saxons, hurling a huge stone which killed the Saxon chief, but was mortally wounded:

> '...His pond'rous course indents the ground.
> The peasant finds him on the heath,
> And in the green turf carves his form,
> And while his ashes fade beneath,
> Renews it at each spring's return.'

The Boar's Head

The Boar's Head displayed by the proud chefs of The Queen's College c.1900 (*OPA*)

Another story connected with Shotover is that of the unwary student of Queen's College, named Copcot, who decided to take his copy of Aristotle into the forest of Shotover to study. In the middle ages Shotover was a forest full of wild animals such as deer, foxes and wild boar, the latter particularly dangerous because of their deadly curved tusks. He was so immersed in his reading that he failed to notice the boar galloping through the undergrowth towards him until it was too late - he could not run or climb a tree and had to think quickly - all he could do was shove his book into the gaping jaws of the boar, which, fortunately for Copcot, choked to death on it, gasping "*Graecum est*" ["This is all Greek to me"], as it expired.

It is said that the Boar's Head ceremony at the Queen's College is celebrated each Christmas to commemorate Copcot's lucky escape, but it is more likely that it was served because the boar's head was a traditional medieval dish and that the feast was held because the college was founded in 1340 by Robert de Eglesfield, from Cumberland, who decreed that most of the students at the college should come from the north west of England, which would make it difficult for them to get home for Christmas.

However the boar's head has been served at the college at least since the fifteenth century, with a recent change of date to the last Saturday of term instead of Christmas Day. During the world wars, when meat was in short supply, a papier mâché head was used to maintain the tradition. The head chorister who sings the verses of the medieval Boar's Head Carol walks in procession before the boar's head, which is followed by the rest of the choir singing the verses. The carol begins:

> '*The Boar's Head in hand bear I,*
> *Bedecked with bays and rosemary,*
> *And I pray you, my masters, be merry,*
> *Qui estis in convivio...*'

Nanny Martin's Ghost

There are many stories attached to the ghost of Nanny Martin at Wick Farm, Barton. A woman of that name is said to have lived at Wick Farm in the early 19th century. She was kind to people who came to cure their eye ailments with healing water from her well. One story alleges that she accidentally dropped a baby down the well and in remorse drowned herself, but it is generally believed that she was murdered.

Her ghost appears as a tall woman in a silk dress, hence her alternative name, the Rustling Lady. She used to appear in the farmhouse: once Miss Ely, the farmer's daughter, was dressing for a ball when she became ill with shock on seeing Nanny Martin looking over shoulder in the mirror. A Mr. Wharton who lived there was so disturbed by strange noises and sights that he left.

Nanny Martin also appeared in the orchard when the locals came to steal apples, frightening them away. She was notorious for opening and closing gates and once accompanied a drunken labourer named Green across the fields from Horton, but when he attempted to kiss her, the apparition disappeared.

The ghost is said to have been laid in a pond near the farm, which is named after her.

Wick Farm with the domed well house in the background (*Gwynneth Cooke*)

Barton Ghosts

The Barton area boasts several other ghosts including a large ghostly dog with saucer eyes seen in Barton Lane, leading from Old Headington, and the old cleaning lady in a cross-over pinny with a mop and bucket who haunted the old community centre, ignoring everybody.

The upstairs of a house in Bernwood Road was haunted by Fred, an elderly chap in a baggy green cardigan, seen in the bathroom mirror by Penny Hudson, who *just used to say "hallo" to him'* and also by her son Simon, who proudly told his schoolfriends about him.

A ghost in Stowford Road was less benign, causing bangings and crashings, frightening the owner Ruth's toddler son Rossi, even leaving a large hand-print on his bottom through his nappy. After this exorcists were summoned: Rossi's room was sealed, rock salt scattered and spices burned for two weeks. The exorcists discovered that someone playing with an ouija board had released an ancient 'Rumpelstiltskin-like' spirit from Shotover forest which thrived on human emotions. It was offered rehabilitation back to its own strata but became obstructive and abusive, so it had to be captured, taken back to a forest area, and released where, with no human emotions to tap, it would melt back into the forest and return to the spirit world. The family now live in peace and Rossi commented thankfully, *'The man gone.'*

The Bernwood Road house haunted by Fred. (*Gwyneth Cooke*)

The Stowford Road house where the 'Rumpelstiltskin-like' ghost appeared. (*Gwynneth Cooke*)

Headington Quarry Ghost

The site of the old vicarage, now the garden of Quarry School, was known in the past as the Bogie Garden and said to be haunted. The flames of candles turned blue, objects such as plates danced on the kitchen table and even whirled round the bedroom, footsteps and knocking noises were heard, and eventually a new vicarage was built. The building of the school seems to have disturbed the spirits and the site is no longer haunted. (*H. A. Shatford*)

Old Headington Ghost

In the 1960s the Ashfield family who lived at 33 Old High Street had strange experiences – disturbing noises such as banging and stamping, red splashes on the ceiling (not blood, and which wiped off easily) and things moving around. Two friendly presences were also seen, a white haired old man and a 'cherubic' child. (*H. A. Shatford*)

New Developments

Headington has grown extensively since the 1920s and the areas between the original settlements outlined in Book 1 have been systematically in-filled. There was a great increase in population in the 1920s and 1930s as men from all over the country came to find work at the Cowley Factories during the great depression. Both private and Council Estates mushroomed and the building industry boomed. The Second World War interrupted the expansion but this was resumed in the 1950s and 1960s.

The Council Houses on the London Road when first erected in the 1920s. Barton Road can be seen on the right, which continues down to Barton Lane and was the main route to Barton Village at this time. (*Jill Slaymaker*)

The construction of the by-pass in 1956 cut off the old route to Barton Village and residents were forced to travel along the London Road, which was much farther for those who had moved there during the 1920s and 1930s. (*Mr. Palfrey*)

George Coppock was a local builder and can be seen here c. 1930 with his group of workmen. George built a lot of the houses in Ramsay Road and St. Leonard's Road and lived at the junction of the London Road and Ramsay Road. (*Mr Ford*)

George Coppock and workmen constructing Nos 24 and 26, Ramsay Road in 1928. (*Mr Ford*)

George Coppock's team of bricklayers at work in St. Leonard's Road in the 1930s. Left to right: Harold Louch (hod carrier), Jack Clarke, Len Coppock (George's brother), Charles Kerry (foreman). (*Mr. Ford*)

A group of Headington Quarry bricklayers c. 1930. Note how well dressed they are; bricklayers were the elite of the building site and it is said that convention required that men wore caps and the foreman wore a trilby. However, this was not always followed. Tom Webb can be seen on the left and William Auger, third from left. (*Russell Auger*)

A large community of Gypsies occupied the land on the west of the Slade at the beginning of the century. Cinnaminta Road commemorates their camp, as it is allegedly named after a beautiful Gypsy 'Princess'. She is described in later life in the novel *Cripps the Carrier* by R. D. Blackmore as follows:

'... she turned to meet us, and I saw Cinnaminta. Her hair and eyes, and graceful carriage were as grand as ever, and her forehead as clear and noble; but her face had lost the bright puzzle of youth, and the flush of damask beauty. In a word, that rich mysterious look, which used to thrill so many hearts, was changed...'

The Dairy of R. Brooks in Cinnaminta Road in 1930. The dairyman can be seen loading the milk churns into the Morris Minor Van. (*OPA*)

Glebelands, Fairview in the 1930s; part of the Dene Road Estate. (*H. A. Shatford*)

Sylvia Bawcutt outside her home in York Road in 1933. This bungalow was designed by her father who was an architect in central Oxford.

Army accommodation on The Slade was used as temporary housing after the 2nd World War. The huts were demolished when Wood Farm Estate was built in the 1950s. (*H. A. Shatford*)

The Risinghurst Estate

The estate was one of those built in the 1930s and was outside the Oxford City boundary until 1992. Its name means the 'rising ground towards the wooded hill' in fact the northern slope up to Shotover.

Collinwood Road United Reformed Church

'Collinwood Road Church did not have an easy beginning, for like the early Christians, we met where two or three could gather together, in houses, an air raid precaution post, the clinic at Bush House, the Community Centre at Risinghurst and the local school at Sandhills. War was raging in Europe, so there was no chance of a permanent building. We were guided and encouraged in those formative years by Temple Cowley Congregational Church.

'However in November 1945 we signed the covenant which formed the Collinwood Congregational Church and by September 1949 our first building, "an orlitt prefabricated concrete building" was opened.' (David Munday, drawing by G. L.)

The opening of the Church Hall 24th September 1949. Over two hundred people attended the ceremony as the Rev. John Phillips unlocked the door and participated in the service led by the Rev. A. R. Vine. The following day the first Children's Service took place and the Church grew steadily over the next ten years.

In 1951, the Rev. Tom Stiff was appointed to the pastorate with his wife Peggy. They were first housed in a caravan at a rental of £1 per week and the office occupied a wooden shed aptly named Uncle Tom's Cabin. The manse was completed in March 1953 and was occupied by the family until 1986 when Tom Stiff (seen below) retired.

On 21st September 1981 the Churches of Christ united with the U.R.C. to form the United Reformed Church. Since 1986 Rev. John Wilkinson and his wife Judith have occupied the manse.

The Men's Group, 25th Anniversary photograph 1984.

Back: Robert Young, Tony Dunhill, Bob Claridge, Peter Boxwell, Peter Stiff, Jim Dyball, Peter Glister, Fred Wheeler, Ray Sargeant, Dennis Hedges, John Wheeler, John Coates.

5th row: Graham Turner, Andrew Munday, Ben Parker, Philip Munday, Alan Sawyer, William Cambell, John Crockett, Frank Ward, Richard Wiggins, David Moll, Douglas Moll.

4th row: Roy Turner, John White, Kingsley Vallis, Richard Smith, Frank Hand, Nesbit Broadis, Michael King, Bill Bruder, Mike Cooke, Haydn Evans, Brian Tidy.

3rd row: Arthur Fisher, John Winstone, David Cotton, Haydn Gooch, Jimmy Smith, Alfred Munday, Ray Baldwin, Colin Campbell, Graham Rogers.

2nd row: Bert Hockett, Edward Mullis, Warwick Pimm, David Munday, Tom Stiff, Bob Cooper, Sid Turner, William Bartlett, Jack Slaughter.

Front: Ken Blaby, Harry Badger, Neil McColl, Geoff Young, Bill Wilkinson, Fred Bioletti, Mac Davies, Eddy Davies. (*D. Munday*)

St. Mary's Church, Barton

A view of the Church
taken by Richard Holden.

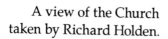

The Dedication of the Book of Remembrance in 1958 with Messrs Hyde, Wiggins and Campion. (*J. Wiggins*)

The Consecration of St. Mary's Church took place on 20th June 1958. Older residents recall that they paid 1/- a brick towards the building. Prior to this, services had been held in a hut and the Vicar lived at 50, Cranley Road. The first Vicar was Neil Howells (1954-1960) and he can be seen (above centre) leading the first Service in the new Church. The servers are Bob Bonney (left) and Tony Woodward (right), later to become Tony Casper the 'Country and Western' singer. (*B. Bonney*)

The Rev. Sidney Hinks came firstly as priest-missioner in 1966 and when St Mary's was upgraded to a legal parish in 1983, he became Vicar. He remained until 1990 and is pictured above at Barton Village First School at the Harvest Sale in 1984/85 when he was Chair of Governors. (*Barton Village First School*)

St. Mary's Church Young Wives Club c. 1960. (*J. Wiggins*)

The Gypsy Lane Estate. The Estate was built in the 1930s and can be seen here in its early days. The London Road is shown with the former White Horse and Headington Girls School in the foreground. Headley Way is as yet not constructed. The houses on the London Road were built for private sale and those behind along Gipsy Lane, Valentia Road etc. were for council tenants. In the distance, beyond the Old Road, is the Warneford Hospital and its extensive grounds waiting for the establishment of the Churchill Hospital in 1939. The fields to the right, now the site of Oxford Brookes University, were used as camp sites for the troops in the Second World War.

Gipsy Lane was so named as it had been a favourite haunt of gypsies throughout the 19th century and was recorded as Gypsey Lane as early as 1832. Valencia Road commemorates the Oxford M.P., Lord Valencia 1895-1917: similarly Lord Harcourt, M. P. 1868-1880 is remembered in Harcourt Terrace and Frank Gray M.P. 1918- 1923 and founder of the Oxford Mail in Gray's Road.

Missing Links

Since the publication of *The Changing Faces of Headington: Book 1,* we have been given additional information which has supplemented and enhanced that previously collected. This section includes these additions and other late donations and is therefore in 'scrapbook' form. It also serves to rectify any mistakes which have occurred.

The General Store c. 1930 at the Junction of New High Street and East Street (now Bateman Street), which was owned by George and Daisy Webb from 1930-1949. The shop supplied everything imaginable — groceries, vegetables, seeds, pots and pans, garden tools, socks and toys at Christmas. (*J. Webb*)

George Thomas Webb and Daisy Beatrice Radburn, at the time of their wedding in 1922. They lived at 46, New High Street until they took over the shop at No 39 in 1930. George was a plumber and worked for Eagleston's in St. Clement's. (*J. Webb*)

Thomas and Lucy Grain outside their house at 34 New High Street. (*B. Stone*)

The Goodgame Family c. 1912 with Ada Goodgame and her two children, Arthur Jocelyn and Rachel. They lived at what is now, 73 Lime Walk, opposite All Saints Church in the house where Robert Goodgame was born. The property was the home of Hathaway's Dairy and latterly the Highfield Post Office. (*R. Groves*)

Rachel remembers going to Hathaway's Dairy as a child to buy eggs which were sold individually. She would ask for black hens eggs and then pick out all the brown ones.

William Hathaway with his brother Harry c. 1920, on the Wootton Meadows between Old High Street and Osler Road, where he kept his cows. In the winter they were kept in Lime Walk where William and his son Harry retailed milk. They made their deliveries in the horse drawn cart pictured above and supplied residents all over Headington with warm milk, fresh from the cows. (*M. Stockford*)

A milk delivery cart c. 1920 from a Headington Family Album. (*J. Smith*)

Eustace Baker 'The Baker' from Trinity Road, Quarry in his delivery van 1930. (*Mr. Baker*)

Burton's Dairy in the 1940s.

After the 2nd World War, the Hathaways sold the dairy to Burton's and on the right are the staff outside the bungalow, which served as the offices, in Stephen Road.

They are from left to right: Miss Brazel, Eileen Piper, Cissy Smith (sitting on the fence), Margaret Greenwood (front) and Miss Ugald, who made the ice-cream. (*M. Greenwood*)

William Christopher Luckett in 1926 of 17 Pitts Road, Quarry. He lived there with his wife and their four children, Doris, Harold, Christopher and Ethel. (*K. Parfitt*)

Doris Luckett (back right), Christopher Luckett (front standing) and cousin Betty (front right) at Quarry School c.1920. (*K. Parfitt*)

Doris Luckett married Frederick Bond and moved into 92, Old High Street in November 1952. They were the last shopkeepers at this address and the business finally closed 1965, although the family continued to live there until Doris Bond died in 1988, when the premises were sold. (*K. Parfitt*)

The wedding of Martha Lilian Morris to Arthur Williams on 31st July 1937.

Walter Ernest Morris, far right, a founder member of Headington United is pictured at the wedding of the youngest of his nine children (not eighteen as stated in Book 1). Walter was married three times and had Bertha and Frank by his first wife; Rowland, Walter Ernest, Steven, Donald, Philip, Christopher and Martha Lilian by his second wife Rosa Louch from Old Heading-ton; he also had two step-children, Cyril and Winifred.

William and Anne Webb outside their home in The Croft, next door to The Swan Inn c. 1901. William was a herdsman at the Manor Farm and latterly a carrier. In the 1891 Census they are recorded as having six children, Edith, Rose, Florence, Ernest, Arthur and Lily. (*D. Webb*)

William Washington is pictured above with his wife and family outside their cottage in Headington Quarry, which stood in the hollow to the left of the Church gate in what is now called School Place. William can be seen in the 1898 picture of the Morris Men in Book One and on page 95 of Book Two, as he was the 'Fool'. The children in the front are William (junr), Ada (later to marry Cyril Webb from The Croft), and 'Tubby'. William worked as a well digger; he also kept pigs which he took to market in his cart. In later years he unfortunately had his feet amputated.

The cottage was burned down in 1941 as an exercise for the Auxiliary Fire Service.

William Washington (junr) in uniform after volunteering for the Oxford & Bucks Light Infantry in 1914. He sent this card home to his Mother.

Ada Washington (right) with friend just before leaving for Coventry to work in a munitions factory in 1914. The young people were desperate to help the war effort. (*D. Webb*)

he Coppock Family has been prominent in the Quarry for several centuries and allegedly has its origins in Cornwall. There are many branches in existence and in the 1891 census 17 families of that name are listed; most of them being involved in the stone quarrying or brick industries.

William Coppock and family at Silverdale Cottage, Quarry High Street, 1906/7. William (senior) was a brick-layer and a foreman for Kingerlee, the builders. Left is Annie Kimber (nee Coppock) with her husband 'Pub' Kimber and daughter Annie. Centre back are Bessie and Albert Coppock. Right is William Coppock (junior) also a bricklayer, with his wife, Elsie and twin sons William (left) and Gilbert. (*M. Coppock*)

'Duckum' Coppock and his family outside their cottage at 25, Pitts Road. Left to right: Doris Coppock, 'Duckum' Coppock, Dolly Horwood, Mrs 'Duckum' Coppock, — —, — —, Sarah Trafford. (*J. Smith*)

Henry Kerry, generally known [...] Todd, lived in Spring Cottage, Spring Lane. It was a small farm near Haynes' Field and there was a duckpond known as Todd's Pond. The site is now occupied by Unicol Engineering. Todd worked at the Cowley Barracks in the building maintenance department and had six children, Charles, Louisa, William, Bert (known as Rufus), Mary (to become Mrs Kislingbury of the Fish & Chip Shop) and Millie (to become Mrs Bobby Baker).

Todd Kerry and his wife in Spring Lane in the 1920s.

'The Kilns' now known as Kiln House in Kiln Lane at Risinghurst was the home of C. S. Lewis and his brother Warren from 1930 until his death in November 1963. The house was so named as the remains of the brick kilns were then still at the rear of the property. It has now been restored by the C. S. Lewis Foundation from Redlands California. Among his most famous writings are the *Chronicles of Narnia* and the *Screwtape Letters*. He is buried in Quarry Churchyard and there is a commemorative 'Narnia' window in Holy Trinity Church. (*H. A. Shatford*)

An aerial view of the eastern side of Headington in the early 1950s before the northern by-pass was completed. In the foreground is Bernwood School, Barton, and the former main route to Headington along Barton Road and Barton Lane to the London Road stands out clearly. In the centre is The Laurels, formerly the workhouse and the Churchill Hospital is in the distance. (*John Bolt*)

Sources of Further Information

Allen, Brigid, *Morrells of Oxford: The Family and their Brewery 1743-1993*, Alan Sutton Publishing, 1994

Arkell, W.J., Oxford Stone, S.R.Publishers, 1947

Bloxham, Christine, *Portrait of Oxfordshire*, Hale, 1982

Cam, H., *The Hundred Outside the North Gate of Oxford*, Oxoniensia, vol. 1, 1936

Census Returns

Chandler, Keith, *Morris Dancing in the English South Midlands, 1660-1900*, Hisarlik Press 1993

Chandler, Keith, *Ribbons, Bells and Squeaking Fiddles*, Hisarlik Press 1993

Chaundy, T.W., *William Kimber (1872-1961)*, Journal of the English Folk Song and Dance Society, vol. 1X, No. 3, Dec. 1972

Clark, Andrew, ed., *The Life and Times of Anthony Wood*, Oxford 1891

Cook, J., and Taylor, L., *A Village Within A City, Friends of Old Headington*, 1987

Coppock, G.A., and Hill, B.M., *Headington Quarry and Shotover*, Oxford University Press, 1933

Directories eg *Kelly's*

Graham, Malcolm, *On Foot in Oxford: 5. Headington*, Oxon County Libraries, 1986

Graham, Malcolm, *Housing Development on the Urban Fringe of Oxford 1850-1914*, Oxoniensia, vol. 55, 1990

Graham. Malcolm, *Oxfordshire at War*, Alan Sutton, 1995

Grant, Bob, Heaney, Mike, and Judge, Roy, *Copy of gp Morice Dancers* Mr Manning, English Dance and Song, 43, no 2 (1981), pp14-16

Grant, Bob and Heaney, Mike, *In Steps I*, English Dance and Song, vol. 43, no 4, 1981, pp18-20

Headington Enclosure Map, 1804, Oxfordshire County Record Office ref Vol. F

Henry, Elaine, Oxford Polytechnic: *Genesis to Maturity 1865-1980*, Oxford Polytechnic 1980

Hibbert, Christopher, *The Encyclopaedia of Oxford*, Macmillan, 1988

Jackson's Oxford Journal

Howland, Andy and Roger, *Oxford United: A Complete Record 1983-1989*, Breedon Books Sport, 1989

Jenkins, Stephanie, *The Early History of St Andrew's School, Headington, 1847-1894*, St Andrew's School, 1992

Jessup, Mary, *A History of Oxfordshire*, Phillimore 1975

Morris, Jan, *The Oxford Book of Oxford*, Oxford University Press, 1978

Oxford Mail

Oxford Times

Samuel, Raphael, ed., *Village Life and Labour*, Routledge and Kegan Paul, 1975

Shanahan, Mark, ed. *Oxford's Hundred: Oxford United's Official Centenary Publication*, Oxford United Football Club, 1993

Sherwood, Jennifer and Pevsner, Nikolaus, *The Buildings of Oxfordshire*, Penguin, 1974

Taylor, Leslie and Griselda, *Within Living Memory*, Friends of Old Headington, 1978

Victoria County History of Oxford, Volume IV and Volume V